PRISC

Nicole Valéry

PRISONER, REJOICE

Translated from the French by
Tony and Jane Collins

HODDER AND STOUGHTON
LONDON SYDNEY AUCKLAND TORONTO

British Library Cataloguing in Publication Data

Valéry, Nicole
Prisoner, Rejoice
1. Political prisoners – Romania
I. Title II. Bénie sois-tu, prison. *English*
365'.45'0924 HV9773

ISBN 0-340-27157-4

 Printed in Great Britain for Hodder and Stoughton Limited, Mill Road, Dunton Green, Sevenoaks, Kent by Richard Clay (The Chaucer Press) Limited, Bungay, Suffolk. Photoset by Rowland Phototypesetting Limited, Bury St Edmunds, Suffolk. Hodder and Stoughton Editorial Office: 47 Bedford Square, London WC1B 3DP.

CHAPTER ONE

The prison's administrative officer pressed a bell, and two guards entered to lead me away. I had been answering routine questions for their files. I had already had to part with every one of my personal possessions: a bag containing my papers and some photographs, toilet accessories, and of course belt and scarf. One guard held out a pair of old shoes and motioned me to put them on, while my own shoes were placed on the table beside the other objects already confiscated.

No one breathed a word. All their movements were mechanical, practised. The officer muttered 'Twenty-four!' One of the guards, taking me by the shoulders, swung me round to face the door and held my arm. The other covered my eyes from behind with a blindfold like a pair of felt goggles, kept in place by a strip of elastic. I sensed him move past us to open the door, and the one holding my arm whispered 'Move.' Lost in my darkness. I was unable to step forward, and instead let myself be dragged. After a few paces the guard ahead of us halted and my 'escort' slowed me by squeezing my arm. 'Psst, psst,' I heard, and someone snapped his fingers. After a few moments we set off again, this time apparently to the left. At a pressure under my elbow I lifted my feet to step over a threshold, then we walked straight ahead for sixteen or seventeen paces before they stopped me. In front of us someone opened a door: I heard the metallic sound of a lock and my arm was released.

Two heavy hands fell on my shoulders and propelled me forwards. As the weight lifted from my back the warder who had held my arms whipped off my goggles, but before I could turn my 'guide' had disappeared, and the door slammed. I heard the key turning in the lock, and then a further click to make it still more secure: finally an almost imperceptible rustle, as if someone had turned a page.

I stood motionless where my guide had left me, unable to move. When, days later, I remembered those first minutes in a new universe, a childhood game came to mind, called 'statue': one child in a laughing group would spin you round, then release you. You had to stand stock still wherever the whirling had left you, while the leader of the game and all your play-mates tried every gambit to make you move or laugh, thus ceasing to be a 'statue' and incurring a penalty. How cruel that game was, I reflected: what unthinking sadism!

My watchdogs jolted me out of those first few frozen minutes. The noise I had heard at first, like a page turning, was repeated at short intervals and reached me as through a dream. Suddenly I was seized by the shoulders and wrenched brutally round towards the door by another man who had entered without my noticing. He motioned me to read the card entitled 'Regulations' which hung above the spy-hole, pointing to it with his left hand while his right grasped the nape of my neck. When he had left and the sound of the locks had died away, I looked at the text of the 'Regulations'. There were fifteen paragraphs, briefly setting out fifteen restrictions, one of which I had just contravened: 'The prisoner must not turn his back to the door.'

I read and reread every regulation, but they didn't tell me much. The following hours and days, however, were to write them in my memory in letters of fire and make me understand how carefully they had been composed. A refinement to imprison the prisoner still further, they even spoiled the few moments of escape that sleep allowed: they stipulated, for example, that the prisoner must not sleep facing the wall. This rule – and especially the rigorous punishments which followed if it was not observed – forced me (and many unfortunates like me) to adopt, to the point of obsession, the correct position even when asleep. This prevented deep sleep and release into a world of dreams.

During those first hours of life in a cell I also learned how easy it was for the prison authorities to control inmates and to apply their regulations. The regular rustle like a turning page meant a constant watch on the prisoners. Every two minutes a warder raised the shutter which covered the round eye-like window and swept his gaze over the four bare walls of the narrow cell. In the prisoner this inspection provoked, apart from the unpleasant sensation of being constantly under surveillance, a state of apprehension lest some rule had been infringed, and at the same time the painful and irritating impression that every glance and movement, however small, was indecent, open to the public gaze.

'Correctly' positioned in front of the door, eyes fixed on the card, I scanned the text without reading it, my eyelids blinking in time to the metal eyelid. In this new and alien situation into which I had been plunged, my senses no longer functioned: I had ceased to see, or hear, or feel the passing of time. My mind blank, I did not connect one instant with the next: I lacked all sense of identity, failing to appreciate how hideous that moment was, or to anticipate the consequences.

Perhaps that was why, for the second time, I did not hear the lock snap back. Suddenly another man was standing in the doorway. Undoubtedly my lost expression had induced him to enter, pushing me backwards to do so.

'Listen,' he whispered. 'There's no supper for you tonight. It's time to go to sleep, so make your bed and lie down.'

I still stared at him in silence. The man leant over the bed and pulled back the cover, revealing a yellowish sheet and a pillow stuffed with straw.

'Lie down.'

'But I'm not tired,' I responded. 'What's the time?'

'That's no concern of yours! Here, it's up to us to watch the clock, not you.'

'But I'm not sleepy,' I repeated.

'Listen, you've had six hours to read the regulations. Are you stupid, or are you playing the fool? Haven't you read that the prisoner must go to bed at the specified time? Into bed, and don't argue. Watch what you're doing, and do as you're told, because every day we have to report to the head office and they take note of our reports during and after the enquiry. Understand?'

What was there to understand?

What I understood, when he'd gone and the door was locked, was that to 'make up your bed and lie down' meant lifting a foul blanket of grey felt and sliding beneath it, fully dressed: stretching out on a stale mattress covered with a dirty sheet, unable to keep your head on the pillow because it was overstuffed with straw and therefore slippery. As for the rough and evil-smelling blanket, it covered me but gave no warmth, leaving me cold and damp.

That first evening, I judged the bed in Cell Twenty-four far too harshly. I tossed and turned incessantly to find a position in which to sleep, never forgetting that the regulations required me to face the door. Again and again I shifted from my right side to my back, then to my right once more, fretted by the uneven surface which dug into my flesh, the blinding light from the lamp, and the forbidding firmness of my pillow.

I could not guess that this bed, like a variety of things in many other prisons I would see, would soon represent a glorious refuge for my poor weary body. How could I know that the bed, with its lumpy mattress – or even without a mattress – the yellowed sheet flecked with pus and blood, would lie one step away, while I would be forbidden to 'make it', that is, to slip beneath the stinking blanket and stretch out my aching limbs?

I could not suspect that the day would come when to sit on the edge of my bed, arms folded or hands on knees, would be a position to be coveted. 'Going to bed' would come to represent an impossible ideal. Anyone allowed to sleep in a bed would be regarded as an informer, and only serious illness could receive the same favour. Within days of my imprisonment I would long to apply as strictly as possible the passage in the regulations which declared 'the prisoner must go to bed at the specified time'. Unfortunately, such restrictions could be modified by the authorities by order of the interrogators, who, to harrass the prisoner, might turn night into day and day into continual exhaustion. On them depended rest, food, and every other detail of life in the cell.

Among all the guard's mutterings and threats, one curious detail stuck in my mind: I had apparently been reading the regulations for the past six hours. I was panic-stricken at the idea of six hours going by without my retaining the slightest memory of them. I became obsessed by his comment. Suddenly, horrified, I wanted to leap from the bed, but this was not allowed. Six hours! Such a vacuum created a thick impenetrable cloud between myself and those I loved. Six hours of inertia separated me from the world I knew before my arrest.

Forgetting the discomfort of the bed, my awkward position and the tiresome light, I began to gather my thoughts, to put each event in its place and to connect the invisible ends of a bridge six hours long . . .

* * *

It had been three o'clock before they had finished searching. The man who had gone over Sabina's bedroom came back to join the others, who, having combed the whole house, were waiting for him in silence. So at three o'clock we were all together once more: the two men who had cornered us in the hall and the three who had been through the rooms. The character with a moustache whom I had spoken to at the beginning was apparently an inspector. He monitored the search, going from one room to another. At last I was 'ready'. Rubbing his hands together as if pleased with himself, the leader said:

'It's just as well for you that we haven't found anything here. There's nothing that could be used against you, see? Now, would you follow me, as we agreed at the beginning: we'll be going to the Militia Headquarters, just for an hour.' Turning to my elderly father, he added, 'Don't worry at all, sir, I'll bring her home personally.' My poor papa smiled ironically and bitterly and said nothing. His blue eyes had lost all their usual softness.

To bring our painful separation to a close, I turned to my parents cheerfully and confidently.

'Look, darlings, this is the hardest bit. Please keep your courage up, and don't cry for me now nor after I've left. Don't forget that I'm grown up! Above all, remember that each of us has a Master who orders all things and who protects us. He will care for us, and help us to see one another again. I'm leaving you in His hands, and I'm trusting myself to Him.'

Nobody wept. Alice called to me, 'May the Lord Jesus go with you,' and Mother said to the agents as they led me towards the door, 'May God forgive you for the dirty work you're doing.'

The image of my family, imprinted on my mind as I left, would be superimposed on all my other memories of the past. Mother frowned so that she wouldn't cry, and, in her contorted face, I saw her mocking my fantasies. It was easy to read her distinguished features: who could believe that I'd return within an hour? It was quite impossible. Whenever they dragged people from their houses the agents promised that they would be back within an hour or so . . . My family knew in any case that I had already been under surveillance for several days. I had even been followed into church. But many friends had assured me that this kind of watch was often maintained on certain suspects around the time that we celebrated the 'liberation' from the Nazi yoke – August 23rd. Such suspects were usually arrested for two or three days, then once the 'celebration' and the massive compulsory processions were over, many were released. At any rate, I had been watched immediately prior to August 23rd. I therefore stayed quietly with a friend of my mother's for two days, and on August 24th Sabina let me know by telephone that the car had disappeared from the side street where it had been parked. I returned to Sabina's house, where I had been staying.

After we had exchanged our last words and glances, I emerged into Sabina's yard with two of the agents. The others had left. Carefully casual, they gave instructions: not to stop walking, not to shout, to look as though I were out for a stroll. In this way passers-by would notice nothing: they would see two young men with a young woman, the most natural thing in the world. An elegant, comfortable car was parked at the corner. Another young man sat in the front seat beside the driver. Was he one of the three who had left earlier? They all looked so much alike! With a courteous gesture one opened the door and ushered me in. We weren't used to such cars in our little street, and I wondered if the pedestrians who saw me getting in might be muttering enviously, 'How happy she must be!' Perhaps others were commenting, 'Look at the handsome lads with her! What's it all about?'

The saloon moved off. I stared avidly at the houses, the street, the people, the bustle: I was stocking up 'provisions'.

'Hold still, and don't move,' said one, threatening me with his fist. Their honeyed tones had changed abruptly.

The driver negotiated the Place de la Nation and moved into the famous Calea Rahovei, on which stood a curious military prison which had been modified to accept political prisoners. A few minutes later, one of my 'escorts' spoke.

'Lie down on your back, make yourself small, and put these goggles on. You're not allowed to know where you're being taken.'

In the sudden darkness I relived a scene which had taken place the year before. One quiet afternoon I was waiting for the green light to cross a street. I watched several old cars pass, then another went by, large, modern and elegant, with several men, one of whom seemed to be wearing motor-cycle goggles. Like me, he was sitting on the back seat between two other men . . . How could I have failed to understand where he was going? But I was in a hurry to get to a concert on time. Today, I thought, many of the people scurrying by would give me just such a casual glance.

Busy with my own thoughts, I let myself be driven round a block of houses: the driver moved ahead, turned to the right, swung to the left, to make me lose my sense of direction. Those who are arrested are not allowed to know which prison will be their destination. My thoughts were scattered, I was in a vacuum: it was as if time had ceased to exist. The two men with me seemed nervous and impatient. Without a doubt they wanted to deliver me as quickly as possible so that they could get back to their own business. Perhaps they wanted to meet a fiancée, or a wife who was waiting at home . . . 'How could anyone love men like these?' I wondered as the car stopped. As the doors opened people came to meet me: they helped me out and led me inside, holding my arms. A large dog brushed against me and I moved my hand, afraid of stepping on him, because I was still wearing the goggles. I touched his back. I heard a man's voice.

'You're a brave one: that's no lap dog, he's been trained to deal with bandits in the mountains. You should see him at work . . .'

* * *

The whirlwind of my memories, and especially the thought of those few hours earlier, brought me back to reality; the picture uppermost in my mind was my recent parting from those I loved. Suddenly I found myself once again in the present, a present clearly defined by emotions of fear, panic, despair, revulsion. For several years I had known that the hour of my arrest would certainly come. Despite this, once the first wave of emotion had passed, when I faced the reality of arrest and tried to appreciate it in all its cruelty, I was overwhelmed with anxiety, disorientated, incapable of imposing upon myself the calm of self-mastery with which I had always contemplated imprisonment.

When the Communists began to arrest the more eminent members of the democratic parties, especially those of the National People's Party which was in the majority in 1947, a whole sequence of political trials took place. The most striking and the most repugnant was the trial of President Iuliu Maniu on whom, with many other leaders of the party, a heavy sentence was imposed. During this period I led a fairly hectic life, along with a few friends, for we were afraid that the police would also catch us in their nets.

Through my mother I was related to Iuliu Maniu and absolutely opposed to Nazism. I had believed that my duty was to take part in the rightful activities of the National People's Party – and had believed so since 1942, when this party was leading an anti-Fascist campaign to overthrow through diplomatic means the government of Marshall Ion Antonescu, who had led Rumania into the war on the side of Hitler. This clandestine activity transformed my whole life. Young Rumanians everywhere, with their enthusiasm and thirst for justice, truth, and liberty, supported this nationwide political action. During the war, I experienced all the thrills and fears of operating in secret – and then tremendous joy, sadly curtailed, as the country was 'liberated' from the Fascist yoke. Subsequently I followed the party, hoping that the Soviet oppressors would soon be swept away, that the Allies would help as they had promised to free our country from shameful occupation by the Soviet Communists.

Before long, however, we were to learn via the frontiers from the West that we had been sold to the Soviet Union at Yalta. Tough years were in store. In fact the Soviets needed only three years to create a Communist system in collaboration with those who betrayed our country.

In 1944, the Rumanian Communists numbered no more than a thousand. After a severe struggle and thanks in particular to their secret police, they created cadres which could infiltrate the army. As soon as they dominated the army and the police, the disasters began: trials, destruction of democratic parties, arrests . . . I waited my turn, resignedly.

Now I recalled mother running to the window, then returning to tell me, 'The person who was there yesterday is still there. It's a bad sign.'

How she trembled for me, poor woman! The thought of my parents never left me, and that night, my first in prison, I was more concerned with their sufferings than with the fate in store for myself.

I knew perfectly well that I was in the notorious Malmaison Prison, where the interrogators worked under the control of the NKVD. I could not fail to recognise the place. In 1945 I had been imprisoned there for some weeks, after which I had been released into the street alone, without goggles. I had walked down a ramp to the door which released me to liberty. On this occasion, when the car arrived at the prison gates, I had felt it moving up a slope. I also realised that I was incarcerated in a different corridor from my first visit in 1945, but on the second day, while I was washing, I established that my cell was on a corridor facing the street, the Calea Plevnei. I had walked past the thick walls of this prison so many times! With a friend who had also been arrested in 1947 and freed three months later, I often used to walk along the Calea Plevnei as if something was drawing us towards the place where so many had suffered. We had the impression that if we could cast a glance towards the skylights visible behind the high walls, it would be some message of comfort to those who were being tortured in their cells or whose 'correction' was still under way. It was not until later that we discovered that the questioning usually began towards ten at night, finishing at five or six in the morning. Prisoners were rarely questioned during the day.

I began to regain my spirits after the shock of my arrest. My thoughts leapt from one thing to another without sequence. I was far from being in full control of my senses.

The shutter on the spy-hole opened and closed rhythmically. Its movement seemed quite natural to me, or rather I ceased to pay it any attention, sunk as I was in my wandering thoughts. I failed to notice that outside a disturbance was developing: doors opened, and I heard the clicking of fingers. After several days I learned that these movements signalled dawn, the hour at which prisoners returned to their cells after interrogation.

A little later, however, a terrible chorus of anguish arose from the neighbouring cells and the whole compound. Men and women, cruelly beaten, lifted their voices together, some uttering shouts of pain, others screaming, 'Mummy, I can't stand it!' It was particularly dreadful to hear men weeping, repeating again and again, 'I can't take it!' Of course, the guards intervened at once, after letting the prisoners settle for a few minutes. They went into cells and you could hear them whispering (the guards never spoke aloud), and like a miracle the silence fell once more, broken from time to time by a deep sigh.

* * *

It was morning, or more precisely mid-morning. Soon the noises from the street penetrated into the cell: lorries, footsteps on the pavement, mingling with the sound of doors in the corridor as they opened and shut. As my turn came round the guard entered, came up to my bed and issued his instruction.

'Get up, it's time to wash.'

I carefully straightened my skirt under the blanket and got out of bed, wondering what 'time to wash' might mean. The guard deftly slipped on my goggles, took my arm and led me out into the corridor. At the end a door opened. Once over the threshold my goggles were removed and the warder spoke to me quietly.

'Here are the toilets. Do what you need to quickly. There's nothing for you to wash yourself with. Later you'll be given soap and a flannel. Quick! Hurry up!'

Within three minutes there was a tapping at the lavatory door.

'Come on! Get a move on! What are you doing in there?'

I couldn't help laughing at his stupid question. But after knocking once more, he opened the door and I stood up abruptly without being able to finish. But that was of no consequence to him – each prisoner was only allowed five minutes to wash, including the journey to and from the cell.

When that bustle had ceased, doors began to open and shut once more. Breakfast was being served. Like the rest, I received a cupful of brown liquid and a slice of black bread, and finished it hungrily in a few mouthfuls. There was so little! When the guard came to take away the cup, he whispered,

'Lunch is served through the little hatch in the door. When you hear the food trolley coming, stand close to the door to take the cup or the plate. And another thing: so long as you aren't called for questioning, you can go on lying on your bed.'

He left, locking the door, and nothing happened until lunch-time. Apart from the 'metal eye', no noise from outside disturbed the stillness.

I got out of bed and began to walk about the cell – three metres one way, three metres the other. The thought of the forthcoming interrogation began to frighten me. I expected to be beaten, and to be subjected to other tortures which I had heard of while at liberty. Little by little, fear began to envelop me, and I started to tremble, as though shivering from the cold. I huddled under the blanket again, because I didn't want them to see me like this, shaking like a leaf. I was so consumed by terror that I could only think of the enquiry, the interrogators and all that such words implied. The courage that I had once had, when I imagined my arrest, had drained right away. I couldn't explain my current fear. I was seized with panic at the thought of being tortured, of finding myself facing animals who would treat me as they treated everyone they kept under lock and key. They would force me, guilty or not, to make statements against myself and others; they would destroy me as they had destroyed all those who had gone before me, and I would never get out of here . . .

A ghastly silence filled the prison. After 'coffee', doors opened and shut once more, and everything lapsed into a sinister stillness, broken occasionally only by a muffled sigh or a fit of coughing. The spy-hole continued its work, but you couldn't hear the warders moving between the cells because they wore felt slippers, like their prisoners. Even the bustle of the road seemed muffled by the silence. The more the quietness penetrated my mind, the more my thoughts assailed me; and the greater the agitation they induced in me, the more they estranged me in the surrounding stillness from everything but the reality of the cell's four dirty walls. Fear, real fear, stopped me from regaining my normal peace of mind – indeed from thinking of anything other than the tortures to come. It threw me into a panic which reached the point of despair.

I tried to think logically: 'You're not the only one to be arrested. You were quite aware that you could expect it. You were quite prepared to criticise those who became traitors through fear. You prepared yourself for suffering . . . now it's your turn. Pull yourself together!' I failed to convince myself, despite the logic of my thoughts. I could almost have wished that I had already spent some time in prison, just to have the experience behind me. My previous arrest in 1945 was quite a different matter. I had undergone nothing there which could provide me with an example of what might happen now . . .

* * *

In 1945, in this same prison, it had been possible to talk with prisoners in neighbouring cells: the warders would intervene from time to time, of course, just so that they could say that they were doing their work. There was enough going on to make the time pass pleasantly and quickly. I remembered the days I had spent here as a sort of adventure. To my right there had been Adrienne, and two windows further down, more friends. We learned each other's names, and we knew that freedom was not far off. True, the misery of the cell was considerable. I was plagued by hundreds of hungry fleas, even during the day. During the night they became fiercer, and whatever we did they bothered us so badly that sleep was impossible. The way in which the interrogations were conducted, however, gave us the impression that we were taking part in a charade, a game of 'arrests'. Were we perhaps less perceptive in our youth? Who could tell?

In fact, the Communist secret police, the basic organisation, had not been set up at that point, and the warders were just as afraid as we of the new heads of the NKVD. For this reason they behaved well towards us. They only raised their voices when one of the top brass appeared at the end of the corridor on a tour of inspection.

Two weeks after my first arrest a guard had questioned me through the window in the door.

'Why are you here?'

I replied that I had no idea.

'Do your parents have a telephone number? They must be worried about you.'

I thanked him and gave him the number. Two days later, when he was next on duty, he told me,

'I telephoned from a public call box and spoke to your mother. I assured her that you were in good health, and asked her to send you a parcel of clean linen. The poor woman wouldn't let me hang up, and asked me thousands of questions, but I was afraid, so I cut her off.'

When I was released a month later, I discovered exactly what had happened. From the moment of my arrest my mother had been telephoning influential friends. These friends, American military personnel, formed part of the Allies' Control Commission. They requested an audience at the Ministry of the Interior, and were received by the Secretary of State, a general. Our friends informed him of my arrest, and let him know how upset they were.

'This girl,' they said, 'has fought with the underground to bring down the Fascist regime. She belongs to a democratic party which took part in the coalition government set up after August 23rd. We have a parcel for her containing some basic necessities, and we can guarantee that she is a true democrat. She is *not* an "enemy of the people".'

When he learned that they had come to plead the cause of a prisoner, the general told them that he would study my case, but that I was certainly an enemy of the people or a former Fascist, because I had been arrested. At their request he made enquiries about me by telephone, but every department informed him that I appeared on no list of prisoners. To rid himself of his bothersome guests he told them,

'I don't wish to keep you, and you won't want to waste your valuable time. Please believe me, I will seek out your protegée and as soon as I know where she is and the reason for her arrest, I will telephone you.'

They thanked him, but insisted that he keep the parcel so that I could receive it more quickly when he discovered where I was. The general accepted it, but did nothing over the following weeks. Meanwhile, the warder had telephoned my mother, who told our friends that I was in prison in Bucharest, and that I was asking for fresh clothes (to avoid all risk, the guard had not mentioned the name of the prison). At this our friends were highly displeased, and telephoned the Ministry of the Interior, telling the general that they were going to pass on my case to Anna Pauker (at that time the Minister for Foreign Affairs). Scared, the general ordered that I should be sent the parcel.

One afternoon all was quiet in the corridor. The prison director, the public prosecutor and another officer appeared and approached my cell. When the door opened, I saw the three of them standing there, grave and solemn. One of them informed me:

'The American Control Commission has got you under its wing. This is what your friends sent you. Make the most of it.'

Some days later I was called for questioning towards eight in the evening. As always I was interrogated about my connection with a certain manifesto. I had quite genuinely had nothing to do with the clandestine group who had printed manifestos against the regime, and in particular against Anna Pauker: I knew certain young people in this group, but I had no ties with them. The story of my arrest was considerably sadder. I say sad, because it made me realise the treachery of some of my friends . . .

As I recalled the thirty days I spent in this prison in 1945, the faces of Corinne and her husband appeared before me like a nightmare. The story was as simple as it was unpleasant. Some months after the 'historic act' of August 23rd, the director of the newspaper *Dreptatea*, the organ of the National People's Party, engaged, more through sympathy than need, Ion and Corinne U. as reporters. They were thin, poorly dressed, really pitiable figures. Shortly after he had taken them on, the director, who had a heart of gold, decided to celebrate their recent marriage, together with colleagues from the editorial staff. The newly-weds received gifts and money to allow them to hire a furnished room until something better turned up (the accommodation crisis was severe, because the Soviets had requisitioned many buildings to house their army and in particular the secret agents who covered the country). I was happy because the young couple had found work and a roof, and I tried to make friends with Corinne because there were very few women in the editorial office.

One day Corinne turned up at my door absolutely distraught, telling me that Ion had been arrested and the landlady had turned her out, not wishing to be connected with suspects. She begged me to let her sleep at my house, anywhere, in some corner, or even on the floor, but at least take her in because she had had too much to bear and was terribly alone. Of course I gave her shelter and shared my bed with her. In tears, she thanked me again and again. As I was also working in one of the offices for the party's newspaper I would leave her in the house, entrusting her to my parents' care. Corinne, as a reporter, did not work regular hours.

Mother, however, did not get on with her. Each day she would ask me, 'When's that woman leaving here?'

I told her that she would be leaving as soon as her husband's case had been resolved. During this period people were not arrested for any great length of time, and the sentences were light, just enough to scare the population. It was not until later, two or three years afterwards, that the heavy sentences began, when an innocent person might get ten years. I therefore sided with Corinne and asked mother to be good to her.

Each evening, when I got home, I told her what had happened during the day, whom I had met, whom I had talked to, or what I had learned. Everything revolved around political matters, because Corinne also belonged to the NPP and followed events with great interest. We were eager for a happy outcome – the departure of the Soviet Communists.

One evening, when everyone was at table, I brought home a manifesto produced by an old friend. Only he and I knew of its existence. I had agreed to slip copies into people's letter-boxes that night. As my parents and Corinne were already seated round the table, I read it to them aloud. Corinne asked me to lend it to her for a few hours, so that she could get it roneoed at party headquarters and pass it out to the young people there, who would distribute it. I gave it to her and she returned it that evening.

A week later, Corinne broke the good news that her husband had been freed, but asked me to let her stay a little longer to allow Ion to find a room. I agreed. Some time later Ion visited us, bringing a bottle of champagne and some biscuits. He thanked us for having helped his wife and they left together for their new flat.

Two or three days later the police came to arrest me. They made a meticulous search, but found no compromising material in the house. I was taken to the Ministry of the Interior, where the inquiry began. The officer heading the investigation had the manifesto in question in his office. I said that I knew it and claimed to have found it in my letter-box and thrown it away. The officer maintained on the other hand that I had kept it, duplicated it, and distributed copies with the help of certain friends in the NPP. This I denied, even after I had endured the long period without sleep which my inquisitors forced on me. For fourteen hours at a stretch I stood, weathering a torrent of questions from my interrogators who relieved each other from time to time so that they could go and lie down. When I asked for water, they refused, and as a greater refinement ran the tap of the office wash-basin so that the sound of water would increase my thirst. However, I did not denounce the author of the manifesto and I stuck to my original story.

At one point the officer ordered the 'witness' to step forward. To my immense surprise, Ion U. appeared.

'Where did you find the manifesto?' asked the officer.

'Under the velvet cloth over her piano.'

I started with indignation, and burst out, 'When did you get into my drawing-room and find the manifesto?'

'The day that you brought it home.'

'On that day, you were still in prison, and afterwards when you came to fetch your wife from my house, you didn't enter the drawing-room, you stayed in my room.'

'She's lying, comrade,' said Ion U. 'I often went to her house and I certainly went into the room where I knew the manifesto was hidden.'

The argument continued between him and me, and between the officer and the pair of us. By good fortune, the officer was by now furious with Ion U. and seeing there were ambiguities in the matter, or at least some aspects which were unclear, he allowed me to describe in detail everything I had just told him. Maintaining that I had found the manifesto in my letter-box, I acknowledged that I had read it to my parents and Corinne, who had then asked me for it for a few hours. I did not say that she wanted to duplicate it, so as not to implicate the young people at the NPP.

But the officer's comment to Ion left me open-mouthed.

'In other words, it wasn't you, as you boasted, but your wife who made her way into the girl's place, and she was the one who, so conveniently, passed you information and the manifesto. So, scoundrel, as you failed to get into the girl's house yourself, you sent your wife. Why then did you lie to me for a whole month, bringing me reports on her activities and on the manifesto as if you had written them yourself, and asking us for money to buy her flowers and all kinds of treats, when in fact you hadn't put a foot inside her door?'

'As I realised,' replied Ion, 'that I would not be able to give Miss Bruteanu the close surveillance required, I devised this ploy to get my wife into her house . . .'

'And what about the manifesto? Who circulated it?'

'The manifesto had been brought home by Miss Bruteanu, who claimed to have found it in her letter-box, but my wife didn't believe her; she borrowed it under the pretence of getting it roneoed and took it round to my flat. So, to give the matter greater importance and to prove to you that I had been to the girl's place, I brought you the sheet and told you that I had found it in the drawing-room under the cloth over her piano . . .'

'In short, you've been lying since the beginning. What about your wife? Did she see only the manifesto?'

'Yes. I wanted to prove that I could work for you, and so I used my wife.'

Realising that Ion had lost all credibility, and that I was dealing with a despicable informer, I turned to the officer.

'Inspector, as Ion U. has been telling a pack of lies, please believe that I found this manifesto in my letter-box. I read it to my family (it seemed very well expressed), and then, when Corinne insisted, I passed it to her. That evening, when she brought it back, I tore it up. That's all. When Ion U. turned up at my house a week later, there was not a trace of it left.'

'Right, but who wrote it? I don't believe that you found it in your letter-box.'

'Please believe me, I assure you it wasn't the first time: I've found all sorts of publications there. I've thrown them away every time. It was only by chance that I kept this manifesto. But I don't regret it, because it gave me the opportunity to find out what serpents I was nurturing and what crooks were taking advantage of me . . . and others.'

Ion U. was dismissed and left the office. The inspector repeated his questions, then he left too: I never saw him again. That evening I was driven by limousine to Malmaison Prison. Here my friends were already in custody: they were charged with having formed a clandestine organisation and with distributing tracts. It took several days to establish that there was no connection between their tracts and my manifesto. When they were interrogated, those who knew me denied, naturally, that I had anything to do with their group. Those who conducted the investigations, however, constantly needed more details and I realised that I could be facing a long spell in prison.

However, my American friends had asked for an audience with Anna Pauker. She received them and they explained my case. Anna Pauker summoned the Chief of Police, who arrived a few minutes later. She set out the facts for him, and demanded an immediate report for that same evening, ordering that if the woman under arrest was innocent and no crime could be discovered, she should be released at once.

The Americans asked her permission to stay in a nearby room until the Chief of Police returned with his report. She agreed.

While this was going on, I found myself face to face, as on previous evenings, with the army commander, who tried every possible device to make me admit that I belonged to organisation 'T', and that my manifesto had been conceived by members of this group. As usual I denied this obstinately, sticking to my story about the letter-box.

At one point I heard someone come into the next room, and ask,

'Who's handling the questioning of the Bruteanu woman?'

'Major Dumitriu, as you ordered, Comrade General.'

'Where is the major?'

'He's actually in the middle of interrogating her.'

'Fetch him immediately!'

The major got to his feet, as it was difficult not to hear the general's resounding voice.

Alone in the office, it was easy for me to follow the conversation: the men in the next office were quite stupefied by the unexpected visit from their commander-in-chief, so much so that they didn't have time to get me away to stop me hearing what they were talking about.

'Comrade Major, what are you doing with this prisoner?' asked the general at once, without even wishing the major good evening.

'We're still questioning her, Comrade General. We still don't know the exact truth.'

'What is she charged with?'

'Belonging to a secret organisation. The other members are here too.'

'Have they told you that she was part of their group?'

'No, Comrade General. None of them recognises her.'

'What are you keeping her for, then?'

'Because we want to make her tell the truth herself.'

'Listen carefully. How many times have I told you that for the moment the secret police must avoid arresting those who have close links with the West or with Western representatives currently in Rumania? The person in question has friends at the American headquarters. Understand? I require an immediate report, and she is to be released. Later, we'll see . . .'

'Yes, Comrade General, sir, at once.'

The general left as he had arrived, without saying good-bye. My major returned to the office, looking embarrassed. Without preamble he snapped, 'That will be all for this evening.'

He led me to the door where a guard took over. On the way to the cell he whispered, 'I heard what the general said. I think you'll be out soon. You're lucky. That man's the head of the police's political wing.'

That night I couldn't sleep. I dared not make plans or give myself over to my dreams.

Towards nine the next morning the director of the prison appeared, accompanied by a guard. They led me off to the office. On the director's instructions I took with me all I had in the cell. At the office they told me I would be freed, and gave me back my bag, suggesting that I comb my hair and wash my face in the wash-basin in the corner: they even encouraged me to put on some make up. I was so surprised at all these kindnesses that it occurred to me that I was being set up to take part in some kind of trial, and that my so-called 'liberation' was nothing but a trap. However, in came the director, asking amicably, 'Are you ready? You'll be out of the door on the stroke of ten.'

'In that case,' I replied, 'please would you give the things from my American friends to the prisoner who's expecting a child?' (A girl in a neighbouring cell had told me she was pregnant and that she had nothing to wrap her baby in when it arrived.)

'Leave the parcel here. We'll give it to her.'

He kept looking at his watch. Exactly at ten he led me out into a narrow courtyard which sloped a little. At the door two armed guards saluted the director as we passed. Without shaking hands he whispered, 'Good luck' and ushered me out of the door. I couldn't believe it. I didn't know where to go. Finally I made my way towards a taxi rank, but then I heard a horn behind me, and wheeling round I saw my friends in a limousine with an American flag. When I'd got in, they told me everything that had happened. The previous night, when the general had left Anna Pauker's office after a short conversation, she had called them in again and told them,

'We've found your friend. For the moment nothing can be proved against her. She will be released tomorrow at ten and you can meet her in front of the Malmaison Prison. If, however, she is convicted in connection with this matter, or any other, don't take the trouble to intervene. This favour is strictly a once-off affair.'

* * *

How my thoughts led me astray, I realised. What a marvellous ending that was to a month's detention. But now? My American friends had gone. Other friends were already in prison or powerless to help. In any case, who would dare to intervene now on another's behalf? Whom could I turn to? In the current climate even your closest friends could not know in which prison you were held, no more, indeed, than the prisoner. They blindfolded you like a condemned man. From the moment you entered the cell the heavy silence gave the impression that you were in the house of the dead.

Nevertheless, that morning my wandering thoughts had refreshed me somewhat. My head was clearer and I was able to get out of bed and walk about the cell a little. I felt as if I were convalescing: it took some time to get back in contact with the world around me. Doubtless the past hours had helped me to adjust to the confines of the miserable cell; I paid no further attention to the regular slither of the spy-hole. The silence no longer seemed so unbearable.

My thoughts wandered first one way, then another. I did not try to stop them. I felt as though I were thrusting a lantern into hidden corners to discover something. As time passed without my noticing, and my daydreams strayed further and further, a feeling of lightness and calm began to arise within me, and as it grew it took on a form. It seemed to dominate and quieten my busy thoughts, to infuse my whole being and brighten the cell. It took me over entirely, mastered me, strengthened me, replenished my reserves, pierced me like an extraordinarily powerful ray of light. It was not painful. Rather, a mysterious joy filled me like the premonition of something wonderful, as if I were awaiting a happiness long dreamed of. A presence filled my soul and the air around me seemed full of a soothing perfume, stopping at last the avalanche of thoughts and calming the confusion of my feelings. It sprang from my heart and spread peace through my whole being.

I had first felt this utter, lucid joy a year previously at the home of Sabina, the friend who had sheltered me after our family had had to evacuate our fine flat in Bucharest.

Indeed, I felt as though here in my cell, I was reliving those moments in the autumn of 1948 when I listened quietly to the gentle, perceptive words of a Christian who had come to visit her. It was then that I first understood a host of essential truths, summarised in a few simple words: 'Man's life on earth has no meaning unless it is lived for the eternal Kingdom of Heaven.' When, after listening to this outstanding believer, I knelt beside him and asked Jesus to take my life into His hands for ever, my heart was filled with the same serene joy, with the same light penetrating every corner of my being, the same power and the same desire to live as I was feeling that morning in my cell.

But, as my thoughts turned to Him, I became aware of a judge within me, exposing all the sins, the misdeeds, from the depths of my conscience and the years long past – all the lapses which had been shrouded in forgetfulness even after my conversion, until that moment. The following night (for once again the authorities had left me in peace), as I lay on my bed in the required position, I began to scrutinise, moment by moment, every year I had lived before I gave myself to Jesus. Living each day in turn, thanks to a sudden stirring of my memory, I succeeded in bringing to light each occasion I had wandered from the straight and narrow path. All the deeds, the thoughts, the wrong and unjust actions which I had forgotten or hidden from myself rose to the surface to be judged. I stood alone before the Almighty. The most insignificant matters – wasted time, a word out of place (not to mention the major faults for which I had asked forgiveness ever since I had first come to know Jesus) – all the deeds which men consider normal and natural, I examined in detail for two nights in succession. They were the cause of a second conversion, or, you might say, the second stage in my spiritual life. I must add that in contrast with my earlier cynicism over these deficiencies and faults, the bad conscience I now possessed made me shed bitter tears and breathe out supplications to the One who alone could put out the fire that seared me.

I could not pray or weep aloud, and this only increased

my grief. I was distraught when dawn broke after each night of judgment. Returning to normal, going through the routine, coffee, crust of bread, then lunch, then the evening meal – all these stopped me from pursuing my rigorous scrutiny of the past. I waited impatiently for the night so that I could continue, make an end, and receive my sentence, so that I could be free at last from the cancer which gnawed at me. From the first light of day I prayed a single urgent prayer. 'Lord, please don't let my interrogation begin tonight. Give me one more night, just as much as I need to put myself right with You. Don't let this self-examination be interrupted – it's so necessary, and so important.'

When, at the end of the second night, I had brought everything into the light (I had made an immense effort to ensure that nothing slipped by), and when, racked by sobs, I had put an end to my self-criticism with a prayer for pardon and for the work of grace within me, an inexpressible peace came over me and penetrated right to my core. But that was not all: I did not seem to be the same person as I had been three days earlier. And I had the impression, which was to last for years, that a portion of my own spiritual burden had gone . . . that some weight was missing. A gentle joy filled a void. Yes, there was a gap, as if a cavity had been dug in my inner self when I swept out all the evil which encumbered it.

You might say that I was living in a fairy-tale. And the most wonderful thing was the knowledge that, however incredible it might seem, the fairy-tale was true. I was no longer troubled by the harshness of my imprisonment. Fear of the unknown no longer bothered me, nor, in particular, the fact that for the past three days no one had summoned me for interrogation. I knew that this would come, but I awaited the moment without fear.

It was in this state of mind that almost without realising it I began to smile at the guard each time he had to open the door. He looked at me in astonishment and lowered his eyes at once.

One single thing troubled me, even during those blessed days. Each morning at dawn I felt as if a knife were being plunged into me when I heard the prisoners screaming with pain. They had been beaten in the course of questioning. The guards took good care to silence them at once: the doors opened and you could hear whispering, certainly threats, before a sepulchral calm returned. But, though their cries were quickly stilled, the echo resounded in my heart.

I spent the day which followed the second night of 'trial' (therefore the third since my arrest) in quiet continuous prayer, reciting psalms and thinking of my family and those who suffered with me. Towards evening it struck me that the spy-hole had on several occasions remained open longer than usual. Perhaps a different person was watching me. You're imagining it, I told myself, because who can tell one eye from another through such a tiny hole? But again the shutter failed to fall as quickly as before . . . someone must be studying me.

Suddenly it struck me that the great confrontation was almost upon me. It was only to be expected. Perhaps by tomorrow morning my groans would mingle with those of my fellow-prisoners. I couldn't pretend that the idea was a pleasant one; quite the reverse. In this prison everything worked together to create an atmosphere of tension: the unknown, the mystery that surrounded everything, the late hour at which the summons came for interrogation . . . and what could be worse than not knowing?

I waited fearfully for the evening meal, because three or four hours later the doors would open for the 'exodus' towards the interrogation chambers. Despite my lack of experience I had realised that the inquisitions began towards ten p.m., finishing at dawn.

Suddenly I seemed to hear a verse that was often repeated at meetings in Sabina's house: 'The Lord is on my side; I will not fear: what can man do unto me?' (Psalm 118:6). It is difficult to express what these holy words meant to me. What inspiration had brought them to mind? How appropriate they were to my present condition! They were to guide me constantly, becoming the phrase I would repeat each time I was led away, blindfolded, to interrogation. Much more to the point, they would be the words I repeated when the questioning threats, blows and other physical or mental tortures rained upon me.

Two nights after my painful meditations a long succession of nights of interrogation began.

Doors opened, one after another, fingers clicked. Then came my turn. I got up off the edge of my bed and let the guard blindfold me. He took my arm and we set off along the corridor I knew. Then we descended a few steps, crossing a courtyard before climbing another staircase. I trembled slightly, constantly repeating those wonderful words to myself: 'The Lord is on my side; I will not fear: what can man do unto me?'

I entered a room thick with smoke. My blindfold was removed, and I found myself standing before a long, wide desk behind which sat three civilians. They waved the guard away. A single chair stood in front of the desk, the only piece of furniture in the room. The man in the middle had his left hand bandaged, and looked about forty. The one on his right was younger. The third, sitting farther away, had a pad of paper before him and was getting ready to take notes, pen in hand. We studied each other. I don't know how long they paused before the first question, but I was intently staring at them, not to recall their faces, but saying to myself, 'Here are *men* who don't scare me, because God is with me and they can do nothing to me.' The one in the middle, who was to conduct the inquiry, suddenly barked:

'Name, first name, address.'

I answered everything calmly.

'Date of birth, place, profession.'

The initial formalities concluded, he added, 'Sit down.'

'Thank you.'

'Why were you arrested?'

'I haven't been told why. I was taken into custody a few

days ago, after I had been told that I would only be away a couple of hours to make a statement at the Militia. That's all I know.'

'And you believed that you were only going to the Militia for two hours?'

'Why not believe it, since that's what I had been told?'

'Ah! So you're playing the innocent. Be polite and answer the questions. It's not you who's running this interrogation, it's us. Once again, did you think you were going to the Militia or that you were coming here?'

'To tell the truth, as far as I know I'm at the Militia now. Why not? In short, I haven't a clue where I am. You say that I'm "here" . . . well, this "here" could just as well be the Militia.'

'So you insist on making a nuisance of yourself. It's the wrong moment to start playing the fool.'

'In that case, please ask a different question. I can't answer it, it's not clear.'

'The question was perfectly clear, but you're pretending not to understand. Pay attention, I'll say it again: when you were arrested, did you think it was a political matter? Yes or no?'

'When I was arrested, I thought I was going to be interrogated at the Militia, or rather by the Militia.'

'What about?'

'I wondered whether perhaps my testimony would be needed on some matter: there are so many questions in the air these days.'

'Which means . . .'

'For example, a theft, or to testify to the good conduct of someone who had been accused unjustly.'

'Have you any friends at the Militia who have been arrested?'

'As far as I know, no. But anything can happen, especially as recently I've lost touch with many of my friends.'

'Why?'

'Because I was evicted from the house where I was living

with my family, and because I haven't had the time to tell people of my change of address. So . . .'

'So, you thought that "someone" had summoned you to the Militia for some trivial reason. You're pulling our leg, aren't you?'

'At any rate, I have nothing on my conscience. Even in my worst nightmares I have never dreamt of being arrested, neither at the Militia nor elsewhere.'

'Okay. We note that you consider yourself innocent and that you have no idea why you're sitting in front of us.'

'That's right. I can even tell you that I was waiting impatiently to be summoned so that I would be told why I was being held.'

'Now, that's a fine story! You're the one who's demanding explanations, and we've got to tell you what's up! Perhaps we should offer you excuses for bringing you here? Quite the reverse: you are here so that you can tell us all about your political activities with the party you belong to; you will also tell us everything about your secret contacts with the enemies of the people and the imperialists. Your file is pretty thick. We've been watching your activities for a long time: all the liaisons you've made, all your plots against the people's government. We have evidence against you in your file, statements made by your "friends" in our hands at this moment. We're warning you right from the start: there's no point in wasting our time with lies and rigmaroles or by playing the innocent. Your file is almost complete: we only need your admission that all we know is true, as it is in any case. The more stubborn you are and the more obstructive, the harder the enquiry will be for you. Our time is precious: criminals of your kind are numerous and we have to deal with all of them. So we advise you not to hold back, but to tell the whole truth. If you won't co-operate, we have ways of helping you. If you prevent us from making progress, you're the one who's going to suffer the consequences. We shan't be wearing kid gloves. You're in our hands and we can use any method we like to achieve our aims. Understand?'

'I heard you, certainly. As for understanding, I understood one or two things. But I can tell you for a start, and you can make a note of it, that I am not in the least worried by your accusations. As for your file and your testimonies, I have not the faintest idea where you got them from. I have done nothing against the State, I have taken part in no secret activities. I belonged to a democratic political party. I did indeed operate in secret, but that was during the war, to carry out missions entrusted to me by those who led the struggle against the Fascists in Rumania.'

'Oh yes? And who led the anti-Fascist struggle in Rumania? The crooks of the National People's Party who sold out to the Germans and then to the Americans?'

'At the very least you can't accuse them of selling out to the Germans. It's perfectly obvious that the liberation of August 23rd was almost entirely the work of the National People's and Liberal Parties.'

'Who do you think you're kidding? Do you realise you're taking liberties with . . . Come on, on your feet! Since you're so impertinent and saucy, you're losing the right to stay seated. So talk, but standing. Now answer me: who led the struggle against the Nazis?'

'Those at the head of the National People's Party, the Liberals, the Socialists and some members of the Communist Party.'

'*Some* members of the Communist Party? And where were the rest? Where were the Communists? Had they been swallowed up by the National People's Party, who wouldn't let them fight for the liberation of their country?'

'Since you're asking the questions and you require precise answers, which incidentally, you needn't do since you know them better than I do, I'll tell you what I believe and what I know. The Communists were not "swallowed" up by the democrats. I said that "some" Communists took part in the struggle, because at that point there were very few of them. Some were in prison, others were unknown – I mean that they operated in secret – and some of those who remained free played their part in the Committee of Liberation.'

'You mean that all the others were in the majority, and that only we, the Communists, were so few in number . . .'

'It couldn't be any other way when the Communist Party had no more than a thousand members!'

An enormous fist smashed into my face. The blow set my head spinning with pain.

'There, take that on behalf of the first of your thousand Communists! I can promise you at least one blow for each of the others.' Then he added to the man on his right: 'I think, comrade, that we must follow a system in dealing with this girl: in addition to all the crimes she has committed on the orders of her superiors, she's completely indoctrinated as well.'

'You're right, Comrade Major, she's totally hostile and treacherous.'

'Listen carefully. You will go back to your cell. You are forbidden to lie down except between ten p.m. and six a.m. You will remain standing all day tomorrow, sitting only at mealtimes. You will think over all the rubbish you've been spouting tonight, and you will reflect carefully, so that tomorrow we shall be able to write down your statements, I repeat, your statements, the confessions you will have made yourself. We know the facts. We only want to check how sincere you are or you can be with us. Remember that you are in our hands and that you won't leave until you have admitted everything you were plotting against the government and the people. Your file is almost complete, like those of the criminals you were with, as I've already told you. It's useless to lie to us, and even more useless to play the philosopher. That's the end of the discussion. Drop the attitude you've taken with us. Either you tell the truth, or you'll suffer . . . get it?'

'I hear what you're saying, Major.'

'What does that mean, I hear what you're saying? What distinction do you make between hearing and understanding?'

'It's that I can make no sense of your threats. You tell me that you have a complete file in which I feature along with other people. You say that these "others" have made statements against me, that you know everything, that all I have to do is to confirm what is in the file. But I do not see what I can be accused of, nor who can accuse me of anything.'

'You have plenty of accusers. Quite a few are your own folk. But later your accusers will be still more numerous, they will be the people.'

'I've done nothing against the people of my country. I am proud of Rumania. I love my country.'

'Certainly you loved it, but not as it is now. You loved it when you, the bourgeoisie, were in power. That's the country you loved, the country you served by working for the imperialists and by giving them false information. You loved a Rumania dominated by capitalism. You dreamed of promotion through political struggle against the people, of entering into the diplomatic service, going abroad, sucking your countrymen's blood without helping them in the least . . . isn't that it? Yes. You wanted to work at an embassy in America, in Paris, heaven knows where . . .'

The major's claim exactly matched the hopes I had cherished years before. A shiver went up my spine as I realised suddenly that the file really existed and that it did contain evidence. Although the wish to work in an embassy did not seem a particularly heinous offence, alarm stirred inside me.

Relaxing a little, I replied,

'I don't think it's a crime to want to work in an embassy. Yes, I did consider it when I was younger. I enjoy travelling very much.'

'Ah, you see? You admit it! You see how well informed we are! We know your most secret thoughts and desires. Do you think we are less up-to-date on matters of fact?'

'Every time you ask me a question to which I can answer truthfully, whether it concerns a thought, an idea or a fact, I can assure you that I'll answer it. But I will never agree to sign my name or admit to things which I neither did nor thought, no matter what your threats or tortures.'

'That's what you think. But we've talked enough for today: I've told you already to get things straight in your mind: remember everything you have done against the people's State. At the next session we'll go through your file systematically.'

He rang. The guard entered immediately.

'She's to be kept under surveillance from six in the morning until ten p.m.'

'Yes, sir!' the guard replied respectfully.

In the same sequence as was to be followed right through the enquiry, they put on my goggles, took my arm and eventually I found myself alone once more in my cell. Everything was quiet. Almost all the other prisoners were still under interrogation. It could have been eleven-thirty, because they hadn't kept me very long. I tried to recall the whole discussion. They had called me 'saucy' and 'shameless'. The words kept coming back to mind. What was more, I found it singularly disagreeable to be spoken to in such a familiar fashion by total strangers. But as I prayed my courage returned. 'Lord, do not forsake me.' That was the first thought which really calmed me down.

I believe that only those who have experienced prison will be able to understand me, especially if they have been arrested for their faith or if they have come to faith while behind bars. I have met few people under such conditions who have been hostile to God. All those who suffer find relief in prayer, whether their misery is caused by illness, the loss of a loved one or any other misfortune. It is unusual for suffering to make you harder or more evil. I have known exceptions, but when even hard cases encounter the Almighty, their souls thaw in the warmth of the Truth they have found: they become human once more, clinging with all their strength to the powerful hope from which springs faith.

I realise that anyone who is ignorant of spiritual matters will find the language I am using sometimes incomprehensible or ridiculous. I am all the more aware of it because I myself have spent a good part of my life far removed from any interest in Christianity. I believed in God, indeed, but effectively as a deist: from time to time I would go to church, but on the whole I lived just like millions of others who consider themselves Christians because they have been baptised.

I was one of the 'hard cases' who met God.

* * *

During my infancy and adolescence, my mother had stuffed me full of Christian doctrine. But, like many others, I had not been able to appreciate its truth and beauty. The upheavals of my era, the influence of those who considered that to live meant savouring as fully as possible the present moment, and in addition certain misunderstandings caused by those who vaunted themselves as 'servants of God', extinguished the last spark of faith within me. Blasé, my mind sullied before its time, I sought happiness in the pleasures life could give me. An attractive girl with musical and artistic gifts, I enjoyed life, and the years of my youth passed like a pleasant dream.

But towards the age of twenty-two I began to appreciate how superficial my life was. I longed so much for stability, for goodness, for justice, for truth, and suddenly I stopped my frenzied activity and began to seek fulfilment in various philosophies. I even went so far as to get passionately involved in the occult. Once again, I was seeking that miraculous water of which it is said that those who drink it will never thirst again. After a while I would jettison everything, each time more weary and more cynical. Thanks however to the irrepressible energies of my youth, I would take off once again after 'something new', filled with hope.

This was how I got into politics. Unfortunately, the mirage of my first impressions and the rewards of those first years soon faded.

I claimed to find perfection in other people, I dreamed of

offering it to others, but it never occurred to me to examine my inner self, as it were in a magic mirror. I had developed my critical faculty to the point where no one could match any longer the 'ideal' which my heated brain had concocted.

I don't want to play down the negative influence which the example of certain believers had on me. I mention it again so that those who hold spiritual authority in any community may know how much effect each of their actions, their words, their thoughts can have. Those who have the 'care of souls' are responsible for all those who slip away from God because of their weaknesses. For my part, the attitude of the majority of those I knew hurt me, discouraged me and drove me further away from God.

So, when I reached the real crossroads in my life, God seemed very far away to me and I never turned to Him, not even at the worst moments. To tell the truth, I was extremely proud, and would never have called on Him for help in case of need. Moreover, I wasn't about to pray to a God whom – I acknowledged it despite myself – I had ignored, rejected, and even, if I was to believe my mother, blasphemed.

Despite everything life could throw against me I kept up this barrier of pride and persevered with my political activity. As I have said, I saw the failings of the movement in which I took part, but not for an instant was I prepared to quit it. All the same, the arrests had started. We wondered uneasily just how far the Communist repression would go. My family advised me to leave the party to avoid arrest, but stubbornly I hung on until it was disbanded and became illegal. I did not want to be considered cowardly. I therefore obeyed the dictates of my pride and stayed right to the end. How mournfully that 'to the end' echoes within me! To whom had I remained faithful 'to the end'? To a handful of sinful men, as are all those who do not know God. For they were nothing but men, those members of the party, though I will always respect them for the fight they led against every sort of dictatorship.

Now, in the quiet of my cell, I realised that all my interrogators' accusations would revolve around my political activities. I had wasted my time in staying faithful 'to the end' to a political party, when I should have held fast only to Jesus.

* * *

A subdued restlessness filled the corridors. Glancing towards the skylight of my cell I saw that dawn was not far off, although the electric light in the corridor was still burning. I was not mistaken. With daybreak my companions in suffering were returned as usual from interrogation. The same cries, the same opened doors, the same whispers, the same noises, then total silence broken only from time to time by a stifled cry or by a long-drawn-out sigh full of pain . . .

I ate breakfast, visited the bathroom. Suddenly the door of the cell opened. I was still sitting on the edge of the bed. The guard and an officer I didn't know came in and faced me.

'You were told yesterday to stay on your feet and walk back and forth in your cell without stopping. Get on with it!'

They marched out. The officer left behind him a reek of bad eau de Cologne.

I got to my feet, took several paces towards the door and turned back to face the wall where the radiator stood. As I walked, in order to distract myself from self-accusation – which might have disturbed me spiritually and even physically – I started to recite songs, poems, psalms in verse and in prose. Certain marvellous passages sometimes brought me to a halt: each one of them I found more beautiful than ever before. In consequence I didn't find it too hard to walk to and fro all morning. Of course the shutter rose and fell regularly, but I paid it no attention. I simply wanted to immerse myself in the mystical world from which I could draw strength, and to let everything else happen automatically. Despite the black thoughts that had troubled me a few hours before, a marvellous peace filled my heart.

The morning's walking had not tired me. However, when I started the merry-go-round again after a few minutes on the edge of my bed to swallow my soup, my feet had grown heavier. But I wasn't to be overcome by so little. I set off again with a more sprightly step, quietly whistling a song which had pleased me since I was a child:

At my feet the ocean growls;
The wind whistles bitterly . . .
On Christ, my rock, I found
My hope for all eternity.
My rock, my fortress,
My shelter and protector,
My succour in distress
Is Jesus the Redeemer . . .

The cheerful tune brought back so many memories as I hummed it to myself! I had learnt it when very young, just as I had had the privilege of hearing the Word of God. My mother and I had visited churches of all persuasions, for she, too, was seeking the true way; then we began to attend – my mother by choice, myself under duress – a small evangelical church in the town of Brasov, where I lived until I was ten. I say that I had had the good fortune to be familiar with the Word of God; more than ever I was aware that this was a privilege I was only now beginning to appreciate . . .

* * *

In those days, Bible reading was a chore, one my mother laid upon me severely, passionately, just as she succeeded in imposing her religious beliefs on me. Her convictions formed the little universe where she reigned on high, forcing her 'subjects' to accept the despotism of her faith. For long years I accompanied her on church affairs, hanging on her skirts or arm in arm. I attended meetings and visited Christian families, I visited the sick in hospital, old people's homes, the poor, orphans, the whole flock she comforted and cared for.

When I came of age, my spiritual state grew worse. My critical mind and acute observation gradually picked out cracks, spots, contradictions in every aspect of religion. My heart grew cold, disinterested, hard. All the precious Bible verses I had memorised at Sunday School faded from my mind. Now that I was allowed to choose my own way of life, I no longer went to church: I cut myself off from it completely. My Bible, with its beautiful red binding, lay abandoned on my bedside table with other books I had loved in earlier years, novels, poetry and biographies which I had read and read again.

One day I noticed that my mother's Bible was very worn and tattered at the edges, so I offered her mine. My mother scolded me harshly.

'Keep it for yourself and don't forget to open it sometimes. Read it and thank God who gave it to you. The day may come when you will want to read it and won't be able to!'

My mother repeated her warning on many occasions after that, always pointing at the ceiling and looking upwards as she did so.

This gesture reminded me of the time when I was required to attend church meetings. These always began in a very orderly fashion: a chorus (accompanied by my mother on the organ), a prayer, and then the Bible passage. Then came the part which for me was always a disaster. The problem was that the God they preached about and discussed was a God of justice, a God who reprimanded and punished, and my tender heart could not understand. Add to this all the texts on the calamities of the Apocalypse and prophecies about the fast-approaching end of the world, and it will be understood that my mother's upward glance and pointing finger were for me symbols of terrible dangers, even indicating the very direction from which would come flames, thunder, trumpet blasts and plagues of locusts . . .

As a child I had never been told the usual fairy stories, and was so panic-stricken when the gates of this strange heaven opened before me, that I wanted to hide under the table.

I have no desire to ridicule my mother by saying this, nor to dismiss her form of religion. Further thought and my present experience make me feel I should on the contrary pay homage to her. She devoted to God her heart and mind unswervingly, serving Him constantly 'in fear and trembling'.

In the solitude of my cell, the indescribable joy I experienced made me think of my mother, and I grieved that she had never tasted the mercy of God. Was she fated to love only a pitiless God? Was this a failing or an advantage? Wouldn't it have been better for me if from time to time I had felt the threat of God's avenging flail? Would not a basis of fear have helped me to gain greater stability?

To tell the truth, the principal thing that alienated me from God was that from my earliest childhood He had been represented to me as a God of anger, of punishment and severity. This I could not accept, just as it seemed totally impossible and inexplicable that those who saw Him in this way could find pleasure in being with Him for all eternity. I considered that their perseverence in the Christian life was something they had imposed upon themselves with an ulterior motive: to obtain initially divine favour and subsequently eternal life. But even when later, as an adolescent, I sought to find God once more, I could only conceive of Him as the personification of love, mercy and goodness. If the human soul is sometimes capable of loving to the point of sacrifice, how much more so must be the love and goodness of God? Surely they are infinite, far beyond our comprehension. The only pages of the Bible which could still warm my heart were those which spoke of mercy, pity, infinite goodness, of the source of love which was God.

How sad it is that so many years should pass during which I offered Him no service, until in 1948 I gave myself up in all sincerity to the God whom I had dreamed of as a child.

My meeting with Sabina paved the way for my conversion. From the start Sabina represented for me all that a person could become in Christ, the Christ who was good and gentle, the sacrificial lamb for the sins of the world, the source of true peace and joy.

Mother had met Richard and Sabina during the Second World War. From that moment she was constantly in their company. She attended, spellbound, the services at which Richard was preaching, and went to every house group they organised. When mother told me about them, I would not even hear her out. When she offered to take me with her to a meeting, I answered viciously and sarcastically. But my mother would not give up.

During the war, the Jews were persecuted and their civil rights severely curtailed by General Ion Antonescu's military government. The Wurmbrands found themselves under fire both as Jews and as practising Christians. The government of the day victimised all those who did not belong to a recognised church – that is to say the evangelical churches, the Baptists, the Adventists and so on. Their heads were on the block, but they went ahead with their religious activities as if nothing were the matter. As I mentioned, evangelical Christians did not have the right to meet together. Their houses were under surveillance. In consequence many Christians were arrested and sentenced, the Wurmbrands among them.

Mother, single-minded as ever, found a way to get me to meet this couple. She invited a number of Jewish families whom we knew well to a sort of 'garden party', among them the Wurmbrands. She explained her invitation by saying that she wished to get Richard to speak to the Jews present in the hope that in some cases this might lead to their conversion. Everyone turned up on the appointed evening. We were to congregate first of all in the house, moving into the garden to dine. I stayed out of courtesy, but with no sense of pleasure. Almost all the guests had arrived, when newcomers suddenly filled the house: it was Richard Wurmbrand with his 'entourage', as I called it, for all those who accompanied him seemed lost in adoration of him. This struck me immediately. Among the women in the group was Alice, a childhood friend whose mother had been converted thanks to the efforts and friendship of my mother. She had had difficulty in persuading Alice to make the Wurmbrands' acquaintance, but after attending a single meeting Alice had attached herself to him and his family. She became a marvellous missionary, willing to share the Wurmbrands' fate in every respect, including prison.

The introductions were made in some confusion, because Richard filled the house by himself with the crowd that surrounded him, and I couldn't make out which one was Mrs Wurmbrand. Alice pointed her out to me: a petite, fragile brunette with a wide smile that never faltered even under the worst conditions. Sabina was sitting demurely on a chair like a shy, well-brought-up little girl. As for Richard, he had won everyone's heart. He skilfully set about introducing the subject of Jesus Christ. Then he sang one of his favourite songs, 'The Good Shepherd', asking me to accompany him on Mother's harmonium. I did so, sure that in this way he was trying to establish sufficient rapport to 'have a talk' with me. I was so antagonistic to him and all those with him that I laughed silently, thinking to myself, 'Well, if you think *that*'s going to work . . .' Several of those with Richard sang and recited poetry. The Jewish guests accepted everything in good part, then lively discussions arose which continued long after the meal had finished.

I can recall nothing further of that evening except Sabina's face and attitude. I have never been able to forget her luminous smile and her humility. I believed then that she exemplified man in Christ. Something within me responded to her: I simply had to learn more about her.

Mother wouldn't tell me much. 'She's a saint,' she repeated again and again. So, one day, I asked Alice to visit us. She told me more about 'Bintzea', as her close friends called her: a flighty youth spent far from God, even as a Jewess; a life filled with worldly pleasures in the company of Richard, whom she adored; then Richard's conversion, which drove her to such despair that she contemplated suicide; finally her own conversion, since which she had striven, with Richard, to bring to Christ as many Jews as possible. In the meantime she had undergone terrible trials, the worst being the discovery that her parents and some of her brothers had been slaughtered at Buchenwald.

I would have loved to talk to her, to hear her voice, because when we met that evening she had not spoken to me, but had simply looked towards me a number of times, lighting me with her shining smile which seemed to spring from depths of peace and joy. But how could I go and see her without a reason? They might even think I had been converted . . .

As time went by I forgot Sabina. We had many worries: we were overwhelmed by the war, the bombings were growing heavier. Where would I find the time to think of God? It was a grim life.

I was to meet Sabina, but much later on. Richard and my brother had been arrested in 1948. Richard's arrest upset me greatly, but my brother's left me distraught.

No one knew where they were being held, but the rumour arose that my brother was in Jilava, an underground prison with dark, damp and chilly cells.

I decided to visit this prison myself with a parcel of food, to try and find out if he was there and to leave the packet with him. A few minutes before I was due to go, Sabina telephoned my mother to ask her if she had news of my brother. Mother passed the receiver to me and after a few words we agreed to visit Jilava together. Sabina wanted to look for Richard. We left together in a car belonging to the Norwegian Embassy, for which Richard had worked before his arrest. I find it hard now to say what my feelings were as I spoke on the telephone, and even harder to describe my impatience as I waited for her to collect me at the house. I could not understand my own edginess. It was as if we were both returning from a distant country to meet again after innumerable wanderings.

I went to Jilava with Sabina. It was outside Bucharest and the journey was quite a long one. Sitting beside her, it seemed as though I was near someone who had been dear to me for many years. Sabina did not talk about Christ to me, nor did she tell me that I was in a state of sin, nor that death dogged our every step and that we ought to put ourselves right with God; she revealed nothing of her peace, her joy, nothing of the source from which they sprang. But through our banal conversation as we travelled there and back, I perceived that Sabina lived as one who knew God, fully one in Him and with Him. She made me realise that God can transform a human being to the point which in our poor conception of perfection we call saintliness. I reached this conclusion in the course of a half-day in Sabina's company, and that was enough for me never to leave her.

* * *

The afternoon passed uneventfully. Evening came, and the meal was served. I awaited ten o'clock, so that I could go to bed if I wasn't called for interrogation as they had promised. I was really tired. My feet and my loins hurt. I was painfully conscious of my spinning head whenever I paid attention to my tiredness, when I took note of myself after so many hours of walking non-stop. On the other hand, if I succeeded in being carried away by flights of thought or prayer the heaviness and pains of my body faded until they practically disappeared.

As interrogation time came round once more, my door opened again. On the way to questioning, the words of Psalm 118 enabled me to master my trembling: 'What can man do unto me?'

It is true that men can do great wrong. And they certainly hurt me terribly from that evening on, and indeed throughout the period that I spent in solitary confinement at Malmaison prison.

My body has suffered dreadfully: my nerves have been subjected to the most rigorous demands; these men have often ground my dignity underfoot, heaping insults upon me. But there is no point in listing here the methods they use to make you admit what you have not done or accuse others of things you do not in the least understand.

Despite my physical and perhaps mental weakness, during that indescribable period I established in my cell a kind of rule, a set of principles, which I sought to keep constantly in mind. I repeated it incessantly to myself, stamping it in my brain so that if my torturers succeeded in conquering my exhausted body – even mastering, to some extent, my reason – I might be saved, thanks to the principles so deeply, so indelibly, engraved within me. It would be this which would help me to keep hold of myself and to remain firm in my faith and devotion to Christ.

This is the rule:

- God is love.
- God will not allow me to stray from the path that leads to Him.
- I am in prison because Jesus has prepared me a place of blessing, where I may be purified, where my faith may be strengthened and I may be spiritually enriched.
- I must never pray to be delivered from suffering or even from the death sentence. Just as the silversmith holds a nugget of silver in flame to create a work of art, and must grip it in his tongs, not removing it from the fire until the very moment when it is sufficiently malleable to be worked, so Jesus will make me remain in the crucible of suffering until I am ready to be shaped according to His design. He has called me to serve Him in prison and I will wait in submission for Him to mould me. Like the silversmith, He will draw me back from the pains of His powerful tongs when He considers me ready to be totally transformed in accordance with His will.
- The Lord never allows a test beyond what we can

bear. Therefore I must never say, 'I can stand it no longer', or 'Let me go'.

– I must take advantage of the time I spend here behind bars to change spiritually, to be useful to others, to learn patience, the value of sacrifice for one's neighbour: I must learn never to harbour the least vestige of hatred towards those who torture me.

Sometimes a thought tormented me: How and with what will I be able to help others, when I myself am taking my first tentative steps along this road, with neither the experience nor the knowledge to lead a soul to the Lord? But at once I would remember the day when, as I awaited arrest (I was already being watched), Alice told me encouragingly: 'If Jesus allows you to be arrested He has need of you in prison.' Then, after I had shared with her the fear that I would not know how to lead others to Jesus, and after we had prayed together, we opened the Bible to look for a word of encouragement and we happened upon Jeremiah 1:6–9: 'Then said I, "Ah, Lord God! behold, I cannot speak; for I am a child." But the Lord said unto me, "Say not, that I am a child; for thou shalt go to all that I shall send thee, and whatsoever I command thee thou shalt speak. Be not afraid of their faces, for I am with thee to deliver thee," saith the Lord. Then the Lord put forth his hand, and touched my mouth. And the Lord said unto me, "Behold, I have put my words in thy mouth."'

These thoughts strengthened me and new energy kept me steady on the narrow way of suffering, allowing me to go forward without succumbing to the enemy or wishing evil upon anyone.

This is not to say that I did not sometimes seethe with impatience for the time when the promises of the Lord would be fulfilled. Whom could I possibly help if I remained alone in my cell? I should add that I never had the opportunity to slip in a single word to the interrogators about the existence of God and the imperative need for them to turn to Him. I scarcely managed to tell them that I believed in God and that it was He who gave me the strength to endure. For, as I have already said, they were amazed that I could hold out through so many trials.

As for the guards, how could I be of any use to them? Later I learned that they would refer to me as 'the mad woman in Twenty-four' (my cell number). 'Mad', because right from the start I smiled at them, because looking through the peephole they saw my lips move, because as the questioning became more intense they sometimes heard me sing under my breath and saw the radiant look on my face – all this at times when my exhaustion and my suffering were such that they could feel it themselves. Despite all this I was never any more to them than 'the mad woman in Twenty-four'. They never guessed, and I was never able to tell them, that despite the pain in my body, my spirit was upheld by a sense of serenity and joy. I never managed to let them know that I felt no hatred towards them, indeed that I was trying to love them and that I was praying for them with love, even as they were throwing buckets of water over me to bring me round when I passed out, or threatening to beat me when I could not take another step.

One night, one of the interrogators, the hardest, screamed in my face, 'If you don't tell us the truth we'll flay you alive!'

'As God wills it,' I replied.

'What? God? We've done away with Him and all the rubbish of those who believed in Him. I'm God now. I'm in command here, not God.'

He shouted abuse at me till morning, and in his filthy language found an immense and varied store of words to vilify God and everything sacred. I have never been as terrified as I was that night. I felt guilty that by what I had said I had provoked this man to hatred and blasphemy against his Creator.

There had been another occasion, although in a more agreeable setting, on which I had heard someone railing in the same way against God. These varied forms of blasphemy filled my soul with a terrible sadness. It was one evening at Sabina's house. I started walking up and down my cell once more as I thought back to that evening . . .

* * *

We were sitting around the table studying the Word of God. Suddenly the door bell in the hall rang twice. It was too late for it to be a friendly visit. We glanced at each other, as if to ask, 'Which of us will be arrested this time?' I imagined myself running to open the door to the officers and saying, 'I was waiting for you.' It's my turn to go now, I thought, to disappear like so many others into the unknown world of prison, leaving my family and friends. When would I see them again?

I was so wrapped up in my thoughts that I didn't notice that my friend was already at the door. She came back into the room in which we were sitting. She was not alone: beside her stood a man of indeterminate age, of medium height, thin, his hair cropped short, his staring eyes fearful and distrustful.

Sabina said, 'Do sit down. This man has brought news for us from the prison he has just left.' Then, turning to him, 'Please consider yourself among friends.' Our wretched guest sat down with the same dejected expression.

His story was just like thousands of others: arrested, jostled, incarcerated, terrorised for no reason at all. Taken from his home for an hour, he returned four years later. Why did they arrest him? Because they had cooked up some story that he had been spying on behalf of the imperialists. In his position as a journalist he was in contact, professionally, with members of the foreign press. That earned him rigorous questioning by night in a special prison run by the NKVD, unimaginable tortures to drag out of him compromising statements.

He spoke for a long time, but I soon stopped listening, as I was overcome with dizziness. He spoke rapidly and repeated again and again the name of the prison where the Soviets conducted their enquiries. Our friends slid discreetly away one by one. When he realised he was alone with three women, one of whom was Alice, a friend of the household, he dared to pass on the message entrusted to him by Sabina's husband.

To put it briefly, shortly before he was freed he had been moved from the NKVD prison to the chambers beneath the Ministry of the Interior. There he met Richard and in fact shared his cell. He went on to give us all the relevant details, assuring us that Sabina's husband was neither ill-treated, sick, hungry nor sad. What could we say? We understood that the reality was utterly at odds with this pleasant description . . . our unexpected visitor had been savagely tortured, and here he was claiming that Richard was enjoying far better treatment. What a naïve, well-intentioned falsehood! However, we let him continue, recognising the risk he had taken in coming to see us and the trouble he was taking to encourage us. After all, the important thing was that my friend's husband was alive.

'Praise God!' said Sabina spontaneously, smiling gently. 'Let's thank Him together that you've been freed and for the news you've brought us. May God bless you.'

The man jumped angrily to his feet.

'Madam, I know you're Christian fanatics, but please don't force me to real discourtesy. Don't talk to me of God. I don't believe in Him. I don't believe in God. God doesn't exist.'

His sunken eyes dilated, his lifeless countenance lit up, the flaccid skin of his face began to tremble; on his pale forehead the veins swelled until it seemed they would burst. Where does he get the strength? I wondered in amazement. A few moments before his voice had been husky, everything within him seemed to have been utterly drained away by four years of suffering. How he had changed!

'Listen, sir, you must not hold it against us if we believe in God,' replied my friend in the same soothing voice.

'I don't hold it against you, madam. Worse than that: you make me livid! You're in hell right now, with a husband in the cellars of the Ministry of Death. You yourself are half a prisoner, and you still refuse to give up your degrading grovelling before your God. You worship and give thanks to a God who doesn't exist! It's despicable, particularly in you intellectuals. Your attitude is just as cowardly as it is revolting. The only god there is, my god, is hatred and revenge. That's the god who kept me going in prison; he gave me the strength to endure all those years in the calvary of cell Twenty-four. You've heard of cell Twenty-four, haven't you? Let me tell you that all of us, more often than we realise, are servants of this god. Because we all hate each other; because we are waiting impatiently for the day when history will allow us to put our beliefs into practice by inflicting on those who have beaten us still more hideous penalties.'

'If I understand you correctly,' said Sabina, 'you might portray your creed in terms of a wheel which allows the different devotees of your "faith" in turn to wreak their vengeance. If that is the case, what will you do when time returns you to prison once more?'

'We'll try to get back to the top of the wheel.'

'But look, sir, let's talk seriously,' I said. 'Have you never felt, despite your hatred, how small and weak you are, and how your rancour and the thirst for revenge turn you into something vile and worthless? Have you never glimpsed that quiet recess of your soul which God has marked for ever with His seal, the seal of Love, of thirst for Him, of the need to bow before Him and to submit to His will? Have you never thought of asking Him for faith and wisdom?'

'Whom should I ask for wisdom? Empty space?'

'But what if He did exist? . . . because He *does* exist and He is hearing every word you say. You said that you were released by a miracle. In that case . . .'

'"By a miracle" is just a picturesque way of putting it. I meant that the police let me go for no reason that I could understand. But you know as well as I do that the decisions of a revolutionary government have nothing to do with logic. That's what I call a miracle: a lack of logic which benefits me. A coincidence! As for your God, I resent your giving Him your faith and your energy. In any case, you are the unfortunate ones, because if you look matters in the face, who is it that you are worshipping so naïvely? An unjust God, powerless but implacable, a God who wields a whip and lashes all the more those who believe in Him. I feel sorry for you, ladies, when I see how much you are under the thumb of your divine tyrant.'

'Be quiet! I order you! That's more than enough!' shouted Sabina suddenly. 'You're committing blasphemy, and I'm afraid for you. Be quiet and let's have a moment's silence to calm ourselves.'

The man bowed his head, but the scorn did not leave his face. The three of us, who had seen his anger, asked God to pardon him.

A few moments later he got up to leave.

Sabina, calm and smiling, held out her hand to him and told him that he would always be welcome.

'I must ask you to forgive me,' he said. 'I've hurt you. I know, I'm violent, my nerves are all on the surface. I'm constantly in a state of turmoil: I'm trying to find my way in a life that's starting afresh . . .'

'A new life with an old soul?' ventured Alice timidly.

'In any case,' Sabina whispered to him as he left, 'God exists and He loves you. It's thanks to Him that you are free, that you've been saved from prison. He is simply waiting for you to repent so that He can give you His peace.'

The man looked back at us till he disappeared into the night. His eyes gleamed strangely.

'Bintzea, do you know who that man was?'

'He's called Gregory Antropomovitch. That's all I know.'

'I've never heard the name.'

'He must have foreign ancestry.'

* * *

In the cell at Malmaison Prison the day passed slowly. From time to time the distant sound of church bells, the voices of children in the playground of a school nearby, or the rare sound of a car broke the tomb-like silence.

Suddenly a kind of vertigo, a treacherous weakness overcame me, as if I had been poisoned. My legs refused to move and I stood quite motionless in the middle of the cell. At once the guard whistled through the spy-hole.

'Move! Move!'

I couldn't move another inch. My will was powerless. My head throbbed. My hands trembled as they hung beside me.

'Move! Move! Move!'

The guard was there already. He came up and shook me, tried to shift me from the point where I had stopped. It was useless. He went out in search of a bucket of water.

With a supreme effort I started walking once more. One step, then another, a third . . . return to the wall, then back to the door. The guard was already in the corridor. I 'felt' his evil eye behind the spy-hole. But a huge weight dragged at my feet once again, and I could no longer tell whether I was walking or standing still.

'Lord, let me know that You are hearing my prayer. Make me understand that you are hearing me. That You are there.'

I found myself at the wall. I leaned my forehead against it: it was pleasantly cold. Its freshness revived me immediately.

'Move!' hissed the guard, and I set off once more towards the door. When I laid my forehead against the white wall again a wave of light and happiness suddenly washed over me. My eyes, which had been fogged with weariness, clearly saw lettering on the wall below where my forehead rested, absorbing its coolness. Words had been cut into the lime. 'Lord,' I read, 'Lord, You alone give me strength. You alone can deliver me.'

Recovering, I continued my walk with considerable physical pain but in ecstasy at having been able to read – for the first time since my arrest – words which resembled a prayer.

My strength returned during the meal, when I was allowed to drink my soup sitting down. After I had eaten, I sprang up toward the wall to see those wonderful words again. There they were lightly engraved; but then I noticed in amazement a signature a little lower down and to the right of those marvellous lines. It was that of Gregory Antropomovitch.

Years later, released from prison and seeking some trace of Gregory, I learnt that he had been shot dead in the course of a fight between partisans and the Communist police.

Had he gone into the mountains to seek the God who had freed him in response to his prayers, or to fight in the name of the hatred which gnawed him?

God alone knows.

The image of Gregory Antropomovitch obsessed me for much of that day, as did the blasphemies which my inquisitors hurled against Heaven. I was terribly concerned about them, because every one of their souls was in danger of perdition. I tried to pray for them, but I was no longer so able to pray as before. An unfamiliar impatience and edginess dominated me. Then my physical strength left me completely: I didn't come to until a man in a white shirt waved a pad of cotton wool soaked in ether under my nose. When I regained consciousness the prison doctor told me: 'I'm going to ask the authorities to leave you in bed until you're better. I'm also asking for better food: you're very weak.'

'Thank you,' I murmured.

That evening I was not called for interrogation, and still better, the meal proved more substantial: in addition to the soup thickened with chunks of potato I was given some stewed smoked prunes, but I was so exhausted that I couldn't manage to eat them. The guard brought the food into the cell as that evening I was unable to get off the bed. When he came to retrieve the dish and the cup of stewed fruit, he said:

'Why aren't you eating? Do you want me to report you?'

'I don't want to eat. I'm too tired.'

'At least you could finish the prunes.'

'At the moment I just can't,' I replied gently. 'But leave the cup till tomorrow, perhaps I'll manage to swallow them then.'

'Swallow them? But prunes have stones – or don't you know even that?' He moved off, leaving the cup on the table.

I was unaware of the night's passing. I could hardly get up when it was my turn to wash. My feet were swollen: shoes were out of the question, and I had been going barefoot for some days now. For breakfast I was given more bread and milk, which I ate, forgetting the cup of stewed fruit on the little table – the milk had been brought me in bed.

'Thank you, Lord, for this relief,' I said spontaneously. Feeling a little stronger, and keen to recover, I moved to the table and ate the fruit, that is to say I drank the juice, leaving the prunes at the bottom. I then attempted a few steps, feeling completely numb. I looked afresh at the prayer of Gregory Antropomovitch beside the heating pipes. How much these words scratched on the wall meant to me! If they had helped me, how many more of his successors in the cell before me had benefited spiritually from these lines?

Then I had the idea of carving some words from Scripture on the wall as well, perhaps prayers and psalms. What could I carve them with? This way, even without direct contact with my companions in suffering, there was a chance that those who would succeed me in this cell might find consolation in the inscription. What would I write with?

The guard opened the door and came in with the doctor.

'How are you?' asked the latter.

'I feel a bit dazed, and I've got cramps in my legs, although they are also swollen.'

'Why don't you stay quietly on your bed, now that you've got a period of respite?'

'I feel I need to walk to get the circulation back into my

legs, and I can't stay lying down; I ache all over.'

'Why didn't you eat the prunes?'

'I will eat them, thank you.'

'I'll be sending you medicines to help you recover more quickly.'

'Yes, more quickly. Those gentlemen at the enquiry want me back . . .'

'Listen, there's no point in arguing with me. My job is to look after you, nothing more. You've got forty-eight hours' rest. Be reasonable and make the most of them, because you've already had twelve.'

After the guard and the doctor had left, I turned my attention to the famous prunes. I say 'famous', first because they attached such importance to them, a sign of how rare such delicacies were in this prison; but also because as I swallowed them rapidly I found a way of putting my plan into effect. Only the stones remained at the bottom of the cup: well, I would try to use them to 'write' on the wall.

I was sure that one day I would leave the cell. I would get moved elsewhere, or dragged into some farce of a trial they had set up; I might even have to die, but not without helping someone. And here was everything I needed to pass on spiritual weapons to my successors between these four walls. So I carefully chose the most pointed stone and hid it under my pillow to dry. Then I stretched out on the bed until the next meal. In the meantime I was brought some powdered medicine which I had to swallow as the guard looked on. I lay down again for a welcome and refreshing rest.

I was consumed with the desire to start my task, but it was impossible: I had to submit to the privilege of staying stretched out. The most extraordinary aspect was that though I had been utterly exhausted until this point, and though I had often dreamed of being able to lie down, I now seemed to feel new strength growing within me as I thought of the work to be done, new strength which urged me to make a start. But that would have been unwise and quite nonsensical. So I spent those few hours of rest in prayer, nothing but prayer. After so many days of wakefulness, of routine, of miseries, of bad treatment, of interrogation in the blinding light of a strong lamp, after insults, curses, threats, the lack of rest, and an interminable series of days overflowing with physical and mental torture, I could finally relax.

The only effort I allowed myself was to sharpen the stone against the iron bedstead, trying to work on the longer side so that when it was rubbed against the wall it would not remove the lime which covered it. I scraped away from the moment the spy-hole closed until I heard the guard returning. In solitude the ear grows more acute, and in the grim silence of the corridor I could sense the slightest movement.

After two nights of 'rest and refreshment' the enquiries began once more. When, the following morning, I was brought back to my cell with the others, to the accompaniment of innumerable cries of anguish which would have touched the heart of a beast, I resumed my punishing round. My inquisitors heaped insults upon me as they realised that, despite the enormous favour of forty-eight hours' rest, I was sticking fast to my initial claims.

I started out, paying no attention to the horrible pains that the routine had brought on: my feet and my whole body still hurt me, and my head remained muzzy after hours of interrogation. On the end wall, near the words Gregory Antropomovitch had inscribed, I scratched: 'God hears the prayer of the innocent.' A little further on I added: 'Innocence is got by penitence, by acknowledging from the depths of one's heart every past sin.'

So I went from one verse to another, with fragments from the Psalms, prayers of the saints, little thoughts and words of advice concerning the wonderful coming of Jesus. Each phrase was written with all the warmth and sincerity of someone who had been through every passing phase in the search for and submission to God, and I dared to hope that those words might sink into the hearts of those who would enter the cell, to live like me from moment to terrible moment – perhaps the worst of my life, for there is no limit to the worst, especially at the hands of militant atheists.

All the same, I couldn't inscribe too many texts, so I took pains to select the most essential from those I knew. In addition to the end wall I did not neglect the one above my bed: there I copied out the whole of Psalm 91 as well as the verse from Psalm 118 which still gives me courage today: 'The Lord is on my side; I will not fear: what can man do unto me?'

What happened to me during that period? Appreciate that my 'work' wasn't completed in a day, but required many days: I would scratch a few words and then move on, starting once more when the spy-hole closed.

My examiners grew more numerous: from three, they became eleven. Of course, they didn't all appear at once, but rather in groups of three accompanied sometimes by a leader, who could be picked out by the deferential manner adopted by the others who were 'discussing' matters with me.

Some will find this strange, especially those who do not accept the miracles that God works for those who trust in Him, but from the day I decided that I should stop writing on the walls the interrogation grew less gruelling. In any case, I was happy with the finished product and felt no compulsion to continue. From the moment I stopped writing the questioning began to slacken. I would still be called regularly at ten p.m., but they would only keep me for two or three hours, and on returning to my cell I would be allowed to sleep for the rest of the night. During the day I was free to walk about or to sit on the edge of the bed, though it was still forbidden to lie down. However, I considered this as Heaven's merciful gift – I say Heaven's gift, since before this respite I had accepted suffering at Heaven's hands for days without number. I reckoned that the prison governers, the interrogators, the guards, like the ministers and generals of State Security, were no more than actors in a play in which Jesus took the leading role – seeking out lambs who had gone astray.

I will never forget cell Twenty-four, which received me on my arrest and in which I spent three months. Three months of walking with God. Three months of joy that wrested tears from me. Three months of suffering, but *accepted* suffering.

CHAPTER TWO

On the morning of November 26th, 1949, my cell door opened and a guard muttered curtly,

'Pick up your stuff, and move!'

I realised immediately that I was to be taken to another prison. There was no reason to think that I might be freed. Deep inside I felt that, no matter what my gaolers might intend, God had placed me behind bars and that neither He nor I would be satisfied with a mere three months of separation from the world. In fact, apart from my concern for my family, I had no desire for liberty, and I managed to calm my worries on this score by placing all of my loved ones, in prayer, in the hands of the Almighty. The thought that God would take care of His own, the idea that He had drawn me here to teach me remorse and to give me the relief that total forgiveness brings, made me wish not to be freed, because I considered that I still had much to learn and understand.

So I left the little cell, which for ninety-four days had seemed a corner of paradise, a place of light and spiritual relief, even a chapel. I departed regretfully, leaving there something of my heart and the memory of the splendid spiritual experience for which it had been the stage.

I left in the usual fashion: blindfolded, the orderly holding my arm; down the corridor and into the office through which I had come three months previously.

The usual arrogant official passed me my belongings, asking me to sign a receipt. After making me don the goggles once again he took me by the arm, conducting me outside and into a car.

I felt another woman beside me on the back seat: I discovered later that it was Marie de Layo, with whom I was to spend two years in Mislea Prison.

We were driven, with the usual deliberately misleading detours, to the Ministry of the Interior. At least, that's what we suspected, because instead of being led up to the first floor, as in 1945, I spent the night and the following morning in the second basement, awaiting transport to the women's prison at Mislea.

When they took off our goggles Marie de Layo and I studied each other. I don't know how I looked, but she was in an indescribable state, with hair everywhere, her eyes swollen from crying, her arms and legs blue with beating and her summer frock specked with blood.

On arrival they led us to Branzaru's office – Branzaru, the infamous satrap. He looked at us scornfully, then held a telephone conversation, presumably about us. Replacing the receiver, he told us,

'You'll be staying here until you're posted further. In any case, you're not sent here to fall into my hands. I shan't be locking you up: I'll put you in one of the guards' overnight rooms.'

We had grown used to asking no questions, so we both kept quiet.

'Don't you want to know where you're going? That doesn't surprise me in your case, scabby old sheep, but what about you, little one? Why, my lamb, doesn't the future interest you?'

'Certainly, but I know that the future depends on God alone. So I'll wait for His decision.'

'You an Adventist?'

'Why should I be?'

'They're always mumbling something about God.'

'I'm Orthodox, and like other Christians I believe that

man is in the hands of God, who rules over his fate and over the future.'

'Well, you can keep a God like that, if He lets you lie around in prison.'

All of a sudden my thoughts lighted upon Gregory. I prayed 'Lord, have pity on him and on all those who pass through cell Twenty-four. Let those inscriptions on the walls bear fruit.'

'Silent, eh? Got nothing to say?'

He spat some foul profanity in which the word 'God' could be heard. Then he rang. The guard was at the door at once.

'Remove the lady and leave the girl: I've got more to say to her.'

'Tell me . . .' he moved closer to me as Marie left the office. 'Now if, instead of praying to God, you prayed to Branzaru to set you free, and if he promised to do so, would you be nice to your new god when he let you go? What do you say? Does it interest you?'

'I'm not in a hurry to get free. And there's no other God but mine, the true God.'

'Shall I tell you something? Here, I'm God. I'm the one who beats prisoners until they go out of their heads; I'm the one who files reports on their conduct; I'm the one who sends them to the "bin". Me! Everyone in this prison knows me, and even outside.'

'I know, I've heard people talk about you. They say that you're the roughest bully in State Security.'

'You've said it! Have you seen my muscles and my style? Who could stop me?'

He came towards me and, his nostrils expanding, he began to sniff me like an animal.

'Well, what do you say? All settled? I get you out of here, and you be nice to me. If you promise, I'll put you in a cell by yourself, and instead of some woman I'll come and keep you company.'

I was alone with this brute in a very small room. He would have been near me wherever he stood, but now, only his gross belly separated us. I took a step to the right, towards the desk, seeking the bell with my eyes. He saw what I was doing, and moving across added furiously, 'Do you think I'm afraid of the guard? If you want to ring, ring! He'll be on top of you after me!'

I knew that Security regulations were particularly strict concerning women. Anything went, except rape.

'It's nothing to do with the guard. Watch yourself: you think you can keep your brutality secret, but one day it'll get out, and you'll catch it. And another thing, don't you think it's the coward's way to take advantage of a poor, weak, exhausted woman? A noble warrior like yourself . . .'

'And you've even got the impudence to mock me, filth!'

A few moments of silence followed. He struggled to regain his composure, because his animal lust had made him pant. When he had got his breath he rang for the guard, who appeared at once, and told him,

'Take her away and put her with the other.' He added, looking at me, 'Go to the devil, you disgusting Adventist! Who do you think would look at a lousy specimen like yourself? Get out!'

My guardian angels had saved me from his clutches, and I was at peace again.

Sitting on the ground, my back against the wall, I thanked God for helping me, before attempting any conversation with Marie de Layo.

Later we would get to know each other better. I cannot say that I got on particularly well with Marie or that she inspired confidence in me. But she was the first prisoner I'd met since my arrest.

'Which cell were you in?' I asked her.

'In Nineteen, at the end of the corridor, just before the toilets and the bath.'

'I think I was in cell Twenty-four.' (I presumed so after reading Gregory's words: he had been quite specific when he had visited Sabina that evening that he had been in cell Twenty-four at Malmaison Prison.)

'So you were the "mad woman in Twenty-four"?'

'How do you mean?'

'My cell was the last, and the guards had a table in a clear space between the corridor and the bath where they could sit down and make out their reports. They talked a bit more loudly there, and sometimes I could hear them, as I've got good hearing. So I often heard: "The mad woman in Twenty-four, she's laughing. The mad woman in Twenty-four, she's still managing to keep walking . . ." I wondered who that was. And it's you! But you don't look mad. What surprises me is that they never thought I was mad. I mean, the guards used to hear me muttering and bang on the door to shut me up, sometimes even coming in and slapping me. But I wouldn't be silenced: instead I used to curse them, the guards and all the rest from the highest to the lowest. I managed to quieten them a bit with my maledictions – you've no idea how superstitious they are! When they came into my cell I'd say, "You know, don't you, that my curses really work. None of those I've cursed escapes. Some are dead, some have lost everything they had, others have lost their children or their wife." They listened to me, and I could see the fear on their faces. They went off with their tails between their legs.'

'How was it I never heard you screaming?'

'I didn't scream, I was too afraid. I only made a noise so they would hear me, and perhaps those in the next cell too. Oh, to the devil with the lot of them!'

'I'm sure it's not good to curse so much.'

'So it's true. You are an Adventist?'

'What rubbish! I'm not an Adventist.'

'From the way you're talking and from the name they gave you – "mad woman of Twenty-four" – I think you must be a bit mad after all . . .'

'I'm perfectly normal. Perhaps my temperament's a bit lively, my reactions a bit wild, but that's another matter. Whatever the case, I've never been able to hide my feelings, especially when I'm happy.'

'That's what makes me think that there's something odd

about you: you're too happy. Only someone who didn't know what was happening would feel happy in a situation like ours.'

'I don't in the least underestimate our fate, but I can assure you that I am happy!'

Marie looked at me, scared. Then she grimaced, recognising that she was faced with something she didn't understand.

She began again.

'Pardon me for insisting, but I'd like to know how you came by this "happiness".'

'Through faith and conversion.'

'Oh, no!' she shouted furiously. 'You're not starting your rubbish again. I meant you to tell me about the things you've been accused of, which brought you to prison. If I'm not being indiscreet, of course.'

'Oh,' I said, disappointed. 'You want to know what's in my dossier, right?'

'No not at all. Those so and so's are quite capable of compiling a dossier which is false from beginning to end. But since I can see that you are an intelligent girl, apart from your idiotic mysticism, and that you have a certain amount of personality, I am simply asking, out of curiosity, what brought you here.'

'I imagine there's more than one girl like me in prison.'

'Very likely. But you're the first one I've met. On the whole people don't interest me: I don't like them and don't expect them to like me. Apart from my son and my brother, I don't feel affection for anyone: the human animal disgusts me. Maybe it's because you're a bit soft in the head, or because you're the first person I've met who's suffered near me. Tell me anyway: why are you really in prison?'

'I'm not trying to hide anything. My case is pretty simple: it's only the magistrates who're making it complicated. Since 1942 I've been a member of the National People's Party.'

'You're not a member of the Iron Guard, the Hitler youth, a Fascist?'

'No.'

'That's a relief. In their eyes, Fascist or democrat, it's all the same, all the same mould. The Communists are the only ones worth considering . . .'

'So I've often been told during the enquiry. And the best part of it is that most of the interrogators don't have the slightest clue about our history, nor about the evolution of the democratic system.'

'That's simply because the police today, the men from Security, they're nothing but a collection of brutes, idiots and social outcasts. They heap them high with good salaries, cars, splendid flats – kicking out the owners first – and the bigwigs in Moscow run abridged courses for them teaching false "history".'

'When it comes down to it, what they get taught is hatred: whether they're Fascists or democrats is quite irrelevant. The main thing is to hate and to take revenge. Hate and violence, that's the motto of those robots. And their rancour isn't only directed against those who urged the country into the war alongside Hitler, but also against those who struggled for years to make the government and the king break their ties with the Germans.'

'Between ourselves, they're just as bad as each other. Forgive me, but in your party there were many opportunists and tricksters who didn't pass up a chance to fill their pockets.'

'Now, wait a minute. You blame the Communists for their hatred, but I think you're full of exactly the same emotions. How can you say such foul things against honest people who are still suffering in the cells next to ours at Malmaison, probably here too in the deepest basements of the Ministry of the Interior, and who knows in how many other prisons?'

'Listen, you're young and you only remember the positive side – which I will acknowledge – the positive side of their campaign. But do you know their past history? Did those who influenced you tell you about it?'

'My father was a member of the National People's Party.

He had enormous respect for Iuliu Maniu, the leader of the party, and for everything he did. My father taught me the history of the party. I did *not* learn it, as you're suggesting, from members who "influenced" me for their own ends.'

All of a sudden I remembered nights when the investigators had tried to prise admissions from me with statements very similar to those Marie had made.

'Why did you join the National People's Party in 1942?'

'I've already told you. I've always admired Iuliu Maniu tremendously. In 1942 I was looking for something to achieve which would expand the horizons I had as a girl.'

'That's no answer. Why particularly in 1942?'

'Because it wasn't until then that I heard about the fight that Maniu and a group of politicians were waging to overthrow Marshal Antonescu's government, which had forced Rumania into the war on the Germans' side.'

'So you went to see Maniu, just like that, without anyone to recommend you, and he accepted you on the spot? Who's going to believe that, vermin?'

'I went to him as a relative of my mother's. You've got to believe I inspired confidence in him, since he agreed immediately to send me on a mission.'

'Okay . . . Take it as read. Then who manipulated you, who indoctrinated you? If he had confidence in you and took you on, it would have been in order to turn you into a spy. Maniu knew how things would turn out: he knew that when the Germans were beaten the Soviet troops would enter the country and that Rumania would become a battlefield again, this time for a political struggle between the American imperialists and Communism. Tell us who taught you espionage.'

'Who would I have spied on? The idea never entered my head.'

'Perhaps it didn't but Maniu certainly thought of it. He was crafty, that old fox! Tell us then who took charge of your training so you could start work as a spy the moment the Soviet troops entered the country.'

'I've never been a spy. I've only taken part in the

underground struggle against the Germans, and then the open campaign for democracy which the party has waged as freely as it could.'

* * *

Marie's stupid conversation brought me back to reality. I shivered with relief at finding myself with her on the floor of the makeshift cell. The nightmare round of enquiries was over, for the time being at least.

'You're dreaming,' Marie told me. 'You're not listening to me. I was saying that it's only normal that your father, as a landlord, should admire those who defended the bourgeoisie.'

'My father was no Croesus. He was intelligent, capable and honest, and he won a place through his own efforts. We were never rolling in money. My family lived comfortably: a nice house, and some land out in the country. My brother and I were able to study without financial worries.'

'Incidentally, what did you study?'

'I completed the Baccalaureat and a piano diploma at the Conservatory of Music at Bucharest.'

'Why did you get into politics if you were a musician?'

'Politics attracted me a lot: they seemed the best way to serve the country and people I loved!'

'Do you mean to tell me that Rumanians really have some understanding of politics?'

'I saw that for myself when I was working for the underground. I often went into the villages, and I never found a single Fascist peasant. On the contrary, they placed great confidence in the measures Maniu had taken, because they knew him and appreciated him. After the Soviet troops invaded in 1944 I kept my contacts with the peasants. I saw them at work, especially before the November 1946 elections. I was responsible for propaganda over a whole district which had already been infiltrated by the Communists, and I noted that there were no Communists among the peasants either. They were all for our party. They helped me to complete my missions. They sheltered me and hid me from the Communist groups, the NKVD agents who used force to oppose every kind of propaganda but their own. From the teacher and the priest down to the lowliest peasant I only met good Rumanians who were loyal to the party and who deeply admired their leader. They assured me again and again, "Tell Mr. Maniu that we'll all be voting for the party . . ." I'm sure you know the wisdom and the goodheartedness of the Rumanian peasant.'

'All right, I grant you that. With the peasants, that was just what you'd expect: they stood to lose their land, so they clung to your party. But you're not going to tell me that the townspeople were of the same mind; and as for the intellectuals . . .'

'Now listen to me! For three months I worked on the editorial side of our party's journal, *Dreptatea*. If you could only have seen the amount of material we had! People wrote in encouraging us, others came to shake us by the hand; from all over the place people sent us information and articles for inclusion in the paper. When the Communists threw us out of our printing works and we had to print at night, in a shop, you ought to have seen the copies being distributed on the street. People would tear them from us and give us notes without waiting for the change; they would congratulate us on our work and encourage us to continue until the victory was ours. This happened again and again, both in the capital and the provinces. *That* was the attitude of the townspeople and the intellectuals . . .'

'I agree that *Dreptatea* sold like hot cakes,' mused Marie, 'while their foul rags were forced on us where we worked, and at home too. Nice lads like my poor brother had to take them from door to door to make the citizens buy them.'

'So you agree with me. The party really was loved, and could count on a national majority.'

'Yes, more or less. But what I never could swallow was Maniu's chauvinism, which was shared by many of his collaborators. Those crimes against the Hungarians, for example . . .'

'That's not true! He wasn't a chauvinist and he didn't commit any crimes. That's nothing but counter-propaganda. What is true is that right from the start Maniu fought to establish Rumania's frontiers. In 1918 in Vienna he took measures and made speeches to show that Transylvania and other provinces which had been annexed by our neighbours were in fact ours by right. He played no small part, believe me, in the signing of the treaty of Versailles in 1918 which established our national frontiers. That was when we were given Transylvania and Bessarabia. Maniu was no chauvinist. He was a fine patriot. He began as the leader of his National Party and it wasn't until 1923 that he joined forces with the Democratic Party; in 1926 they amalgamated with the People's Party whose leader was the famous historian, N. Iorga.'

'Let's drop the propaganda. You've really been well indoctrinated.'

'It's not a matter of propaganda. I'm citing particular dates: when you don't know the truth you're tempted to repeat all kinds of unpleasant lies.'

'I'm perfectly well acquainted with your "history". I've *lived* it. You were only a child in 1928 when the papers were shouting about the creation of the most powerful, most popular opposition party, your own dear National People's Party . . . now calm down, I'm only having a little fun at your expense!'

The door opened. The guard brought in two panniers filled with beans and two good hunks of bread.

'That's better than the Malmaison.' Marie threw herself on the food.

I felt sorry for her as I watched her devouring it. When she had finished I held out my bowl, which I had not yet touched.

'Go on, take half of it.'

'Why aren't you eating? Did they overfeed you at the Malmaison?'

Refusing to reply to her sour query, I continued to hold out the bowl.

'Why are you doing this, some sort of charity?'

'I'm not hungry. But take it as charity if it helps your appetite.'

She helped herself to half my share and continued to eat.

I closed my eyes to bring the discussion to a close. Shortly afterwards, Marie stretched herself out on the floor, where she wriggled about to find the most comfortable sleeping position. A few minutes later she was snoring.

I couldn't get to sleep. The conversation had upset me, and too many memories crowded in upon me. I had lost the inner calm that I had found alone in my cell. My memories had been carefully filed, like drawers, and I had thought they were sorted out for good. Now they were springing up once more. Bitterness overwhelmed me: I could have screamed out loud down the corridors, which a thick curtain screened off from our gaze.

* * *

Many of those who supported Maniu in his fight against the Fascists and Communists must be languishing along those corridors, I reflected. Among them there would certainly be those who were faithful to him until the party was dissolved in 1947, together with those who had quit him during the different proceedings which had been brought against members of the party. There would also be some who had denied him during his own trial, a sinister piece of staging by the 'Security', a faithful copy of the Soviet NKVD. Newspaper headlines marched past in my mind: MANIU THE TRAITOR, YOU LIED TO US, MR. MANIU . . . It must have hurt him so deeply to remember such betrayals as he passed his nights and days in a miserable cell. He had longed so much for his country and his people to bloom in harmony. There was nothing of the revolutionary's hatred and violence about him, but rather prudence and confidence in a political evolution which would deepen, organise and stabilise firm laws to nurture the progress of a united people.

Such accusers would rankle – not just the Communists

and riff-raff in the streets, shouting slogans dictated by the Communist Party, but also, in some cases, those who had once been close to him. He had clearly foreseen how events would take shape.

I thought I could see it coming on the evening of the November 1946 elections. From all over the country calls were pouring in, announcing that our party had won in almost every constituency, and we were overjoyed. Maniu, however, had withdrawn to his room alone. Late that night, when we were deliriously happy at the results our delegates had cabled or telephoned, the landlord of the house where Maniu lived knocked at his door. He appeared wearing the long cloak he habitually donned at home. He listened carefully to the information his friends told him, their voices choked with emotion as they all spoke at once. He heard them out, patiently, almost indifferently. When everyone had fallen silent, astonished at his imperturbability, he spoke, his tones measured. What he said I shall never forget.

'These are *our* results which indicate the will of *our* people. But tomorrow you will see the results published by the occupying forces. The results will be faked, I can tell you now. The party has not won. Please forgive me, I'm tired. Good night.'

The following day the papers announced the 'overwhelming' success (with falsified returns) of the Communists in the 'free' elections.

We might have expected it. The Soviet troops protected the Communists; the NKVD instructors were on the spot, whereas the American and English supervising commissions were not allowed to enter any voting hall. The government had allowed only four Western journalists to attend the elections, and these were carefully shown only those voting halls where the Communists were certain of winning.

Such memories were bitter. As I thought of the poor peasants who had put their faith in Maniu's activities, once again I could hear people telling me, 'Maniu has extensive influence with Western politicians; they think very highly of him.' 'Is it true that Maniu has sent a report to Churchill on the Communists' outrages?' 'Truman promised Maniu.' 'An allied delegation has visited Stalin as a result of Maniu's interventions.'

Yes, he had done all this, and more, to carry out his duty to his people right to the end, but he knew in advance that his cause was lost.

During the years of underground opposition to Antonescu's government, the Western Allies had assured Maniu that after victory Rumania would at last know the freedom and dignity of democracy. The country's state during the war was far too serious for Maniu to refuse an alliance against the Fascists with the National Liberal Party (who represented the rich bourgeois capitalists) and the Democratic Socialists. Even the handful of Communists who existed at the time found a place in the coalition. Result? On August 23rd, 1944, the memorable day on which the armistice was agreed with the Russians, the National People's Party was associated with three other political movements. Immediately afterwards, some Communists, now released from prison – in particular their leader, Gheorghiu-Dej – began to lay secret plans, supported by the occupying Soviet forces and with increased confidence as a result of Yalta, at which the West had sold the countries of the East.

After August 23rd, the country was initially run by the four groups who had engineered the liberation. They governed together under the general heading of the National Democratic Union. But there was considerable friction. The handful of Communists who had emerged from prison (helped by those who had fled to Moscow, receiving instruction and shelter during the war, such as Anna Pauker, Vasile Luca and Emile Bodnaras) induced some democrats by threats and blackmail to quit their parties. Thus the Communists managed to provoke divisions within the democratic block. Bringing new alliances together, they created pseudo-parties which owed allegiance to the Communist Party and the USSR. As the West abandoned Rumania in accordance with the decisions taken at Yalta, the members of the National Democratic Union found themselves separated from one another, to be replaced by opportunists and dissident traitors.

March 6th, 1945, was particularly grim. The whole country trembled with fear. A. Vychinsky, the Soviet envoy to Bucharest, went to the palace: everyone knew that each of his visits had been followed by some catastrophe. (A strange feeling came upon me as I remembered this memorable date in our sad history.) Pounding on the table Vychinsky imposed a totally Communist government on the king, led by Dr. Petru Groza, a bourgeois who had sold himself to the Communists. This took place immediately, which gave the Communists time to prepare the sham elections in November 1946. They were also able to close their ranks, assimilating as they did so both dissident traitors and innocents.

The people revolted. Anti-Soviet and anti-Communist organisations sprang up everywhere. People fled to the mountains for hiding. But the political police and the NKVD stifled every move: the prison doors opened wide and the finest of our people disappeared behind bars.

The National People's Party continued to do its duty: supporting the Rumanians' spirits, publishing secret manifestos, and sending formal protests to the Allied supervisors each day. The protests detailed all the Communists' outrages, the atrocities and arrests.

* * *

When Marie awoke the room was dark. I had spent several hours in the company of many different people, among them those closest to me. I had gone back over events in which I had taken part with all the zest of my youth and character. I had aged so much in those few years! My confidence in man had disapppeared, except for those like Iuliu Maniu, who will always remain for me a model of self-sacrifice and faithfulness.

'What a dream I've had!' said Marie suddenly. 'They were beating me because I wouldn't give my son up to them. And then . . . ah, yes, my brother . . . He was searching the ground in the dark with the help of a lantern.'

'You fell asleep after eating those beans. A heavy meal often gives you nightmares.'

'The real nightmare is the one I live all the time, because I can't stop thinking about my son. He's been left completely alone, without any material or moral support.'

'What about your brother? Can't he take care of him?'

'Yes. But he may have been arrested because of me. And even if he is free, do you think he's got the means to support him?'

'Has he got a job?'

'Yes, in a factory, as an unskilled labourer. When you think he's an intellectual, a former businessman . . . And now he's trying to learn welding in a small factory. If you could have seen the real "gent" he used to be! But those bastards have ruined him. First of all there was the stabilisation of the currency, when at a stroke he lost all his savings. He was so flabbergasted that he tried to commit suicide . . .'

'There were a lot of suicides in 1947 because of the stabilisation.'

'Yes, I know. But that isn't all. He reached his lowest ebb in December 1947 when those brutes dethroned King Michael. My brother had been in great favour at the palace. The king's expulsion and the departure of his many friends there did a lot of harm to his businesses. In 1948 the *coup de grâce* fell: the industries were nationalised. He lost his factory. He found himself without a sou, without a job, without hope. At the age of forty-five he had to start again from scratch.'

'Did he live with you and your son?'

'No. They'd stuck him in a miserable room in some flats in the suburbs of Bucharest. Five families crowded in one apartment, five women in one kitchen, more than fifteen people using one bathroom. As for me and my son, we lived in Cluj: after the education system had been reformed, I lost my job as a teacher and found myself 'relocated' as a worker in a chemicals factory in the town. That's where they arrested me. Devil take them all!'

Marie fell asleep again, tired by her complaints and curses. I stayed awake, however, together with the poor folk in the cells around us.

* * *

After my sleepless night in the Ministry of the Interior they bundled us into a car, and we crossed Bucharest without being blindfolded. We were taken to the station in the north of the city, but we were not told our ultimate destination. Two policemen went with us. We were so astonished at being able to walk like anybody else, and to see the familiar platform, that we actually forgot to look at the notice giving the train's destination or the time it would leave. The guards had warned us:

'Now look, we are going to catch a train from Bucharest North. So as not to draw attention to yourselves you will not have handcuffs. But . . . one move, one word, and we'll shoot. We can say that you were criminals and that you were trying to escape.'

We were both convinced that we were going to be deported to the USSR. I felt I was departing for ever, leaving behind my parents who lived with – were tolerated by – some relatives: we had been ejected from our fine large house. I thought sadly of all the friends who perhaps would never know what had become of me. My parents would certainly look for me, and, failing to find me in any prison in the country, would conclude that I had been deported; all they would be able to do would be to weep for my lost youth and their own solitude. A torrent of sad thoughts poured through me.

I made a conscious effort of will to shake off my melancholy.

All of a sudden Marie shouted, 'Micu!'

But the young man she had called failed to hear her in the

racket of the station. Stunned, she told me, ‘I’ve just seen my son, my child, my child! And he didn’t see me!’

The passers-by looked at us without paying any attention. How could they be so indifferent? Marie at least seemed to have landed from another planet. Her hair, normally fuzzy, looked extraordinary after so many months without attention, and the blotches on her dress were plainly visible.

The guards immediately slapped handcuffs on us, cursing us for ‘thieves’ and ‘criminals’. That did attract the attention of the passers-by, who stared at us in scorn.

We climbed aboard. I felt at peace within, and was able to stifle my protests, disregarding the handcuffs and the guards’ impudence as they sat us down in a compartment next to free travellers. It didn’t worry me to hear them telling the curious that we were thieves whom they were conducting to a larger prison. As I left Bucharest North, my country’s skies seemed more lovely than ever.

Ignoring my fears and worries, lulled by the progress of the train, I allowed myself to sink into a quietness of spirit beyond words. I did not even feel the guard shake me and pull me roughly from the seat: the noise of the chain which linked us must have jolted me out of my dream. Under the humiliating, pitying gaze of the travellers we got down from the train at Ploesti, sixty kilometres from Bucharest.

A van like a black crate was waiting for us, and we climbed aboard with our escort. We travelled for some time in silence, contenting ourselves with imagining the beauty of the countryside which formed the main attraction of the area about the town, the valley of the Prahova.

* * *

We got to Mislea as dusk was falling.

A former monastery had been converted into a women’s prison. The region, surrounded at a distance by sub-carparthian hills, was famous for its forests, its greenery and flowers.

The herds were coming in from the pastures. Autumn

that year was splendid, long and warm, like the day we arrived at Mislea. The pleasant twilight was very still, scarcely disturbed by the creaking of an axle or a dog barking . . .

As we climbed down from our 'crate', we could not have imagined the contrast between the splendid site of the former monastery and the hideous situation prevailing behind its walls.

After placing us in the hands of the warders at Mislea, the van and our guards departed. The prison's chief warder, a peasant with a kind expression, told us to wait for the director, waving us to a wooden bench near the door of her office. I wanted to capture all the air's freshness, fix in my mind the colours of the dusk: I was anxious to store my memories for the Lord knew how many days. Once inside, we would be unable to see the lovely fields planted with apple and pear trees.

As we waited for the director to arrive Marie struck up a conversation with the chief guard, who told her that the director, a woman, held the rank of major in the Security's forces, that she had been an underground member of the Communist Party, and had taken a philosophy degree; that she was extremely tough, with a masculine manner, quick of speech and gesture with a blustering voice: in short, that her force and energy allowed her to dominate more than 1300 prisoners and a hundred warders, not to mention the administrative personnel.

When she appeared I saw that the warder had not exaggerated in the least. We were face to face with a virago: plump, stocky, her head out of proportion to her body; a lock of hair was constantly falling forward across her forehead, and she would flick it back with a nervous gesture. No trace of feminity remained in this woman with her military manner and officer's uniform. The only human thing about her, the only sign of warmth and encouragement, was her eyes, which were black, alive, mischievous and always moist.

She unceremoniously checked the details and cast an eye

over the 'secret' dossiers that had come with us, then called the head warder and said, 'Take them both to the *lagher*.'

As I was to learn later, the *lagher* was the furthest point of the prison, an enclosed area where the prisoners had no contact with anyone, and not even the right to work; they were simply kept available for their respective investigators. It was a building containing two large rooms separated by a smaller room where the warder on duty was permanently stationed. The room on the right was for supposedly 'normal' prisoners, that on the left for those being punished for some insubordination. This was known as 'the black hole'. The prisoners here were those whom the director considered undisciplined, recalcitrant, etc. The sentence could be long or short: once in the 'hole' you were no longer allowed to take part in the daily exercise and the food ration – already frugal – was cut by fifty or twenty-five per cent, depending on the case.

If in spite of this you didn't mend your ways, you passed on to the next stage, the *gherla*, a tiny cell which would hold just one person standing. You couldn't sit except by folding double . . .

The building in the enclosure could contain from a hundred to a hundred and fifty people, depending on how many layers of bunks were set up. Outside, a strip of dry ground ran the length of the building, roughly three metres across. A wall three metres high cut it off from the square prison yard. On this strip of ground, where those in the confined quarters took their exercise, a tree, a plane tree, had survived by some miracle.

The room on the right, then, held prisoners under the *lagher*'s special regime: those who had not been condemned in the courts for lack of proof, and were still held at the disposition of the investigators while waiting for an eventual decision; and those who had been judged and sentenced, but who, when their sentence was complete, had been given a further stretch, an 'administrative' punishment decided by an ad hoc tribunal which took place at the Ministry of the Interior. The 'supplement' was intended to 're-educate' them, as the initial punishment had not produced satisfactory results. It must be remembered that the sentences passed by the 'legal' means, that is to say by a trial, were also elastic, resting on the discretion of the investigators, as we knew very well. In other words, they could be increased or decreased (which was unheard of) according to the whim of those in charge of that particular case.

The fact that most of the women in the enclosure had been sentenced without trial made their predicament far worse. According to the Communist mentality, lack of proof shows that you have carried out your anti-government activities with particular skill, in so far as the investigators have not been able to establish evidence, even by the use of torture. That is why women in the *lagher* were considered more suspect and more dangerous: while the authorities waited for some indiscretion which would allow the enquiry to be restarted in one case or another, we were kept in total isolation. All outside contact was prohibited, even with those prisoners in other parts of the prison. We lived in the constant fear of a new enquiry, which might take place in one of the prison's administrative offices or worse still at the Ministry of the Interior, at the Malmaison or one of the secret buildings purpose-built for the use of methods which would produce definite results. A limousine would come and take the prisoner from the prison gates to these enquiry centres: sometimes she would return, sometimes not.

The rest of the prison contained around 1200 prisoners, from those with five-year sentences to those with life imprisonment. They worked in workshops, were allowed to walk about the yard, from which we were cut off by the wall, and had more freedom than us, but their work was hard, as everything depended on the 'norm'.

The prison was secluded, cut off from the rest of the world. We would try every possible means to catch sight of other people, our ultimate aim being to spot relatives or acquaintances. At one point there was a tiny crack in the wall: if the superintendent's back was turned someone would rush to it, and if those on the other side were exercising the news would come flooding forth, with people calling names of those unfortunates on the other side of our wall.

The problem of prisons had always concerned me. I had read several books on the subject. I had been particularly taken with the life of the missionary Mathilda Wrede, the 'angel of the prisons', as she was known in Finland. I had also heard of Mislea, which before the Second World War had for many years been a strict prison for those sentenced under civil law.

Some years previously, I had visited a friend of the family in Vacaresti prison in Bucharest. Moved, I entered respectfully, feeling I was making my way into a place peopled with ghosts walking to and fro. The regime then imposed on the prisoners was impossibly severe, and no one would have believed that you could suffer just as much under the Communists. However we were prisoners between 1948 and 1954, and experienced the worst of the Stalinist influence.

Nothing from outside penetrated into the prison. It was as if we were buried alive. News only circulated when a prisoner was transferred from one prison to another, from an enquiry to the prison or from the prison to another enquiry. Thus in one way or another we learned about certain matters which might interest us, and from time to time political news would reach us.

We were kept under strict surveillance. Two female guards watched us constantly, one in the small room between the two larger buildings and the other at the gate let into the wall outside. This double observation is utterly characteristic of Communist principles. The Communists knew that little love was wasted on them, so they had the foresight to appoint two people for each job: investigators checked on the guards to ensure that no conspiracy arose, and to prevent our having any influence on them. The rule of reciprocal spying was followed for all ranks. The Communist Party also encouraged informers, a practice which in certain prisons, sometimes with the aid of the prisoners themselves, led to atrocities unique in the history of the human race.

I was entering a penitentiary for the first time. When the guard opened the door we stopped short on the threshold; the floor of beaten earth was filled with women for the whole length of the building. Before we could go in, we had to wait until those who had been sitting got to their feet.

The women dragged themselves upright, indifferent to our arrival. I felt my head start to spin. Was it too many faces at once, after the isolation of the preceding months? Too much light, despite the soft flow of the late autumn sun? Perhaps it was rather the vague sense that I would find enormous satisfaction among these dear sisters, who were to be part of me for ever. Later I heard them say, as they looked back affectionately to the day I arrived, that if my eyes had seemed fearful, my face shone with joy. Yes, I replied, the shock of the occasion had brought fear to my eyes – I felt as if I had arrived at a cemetery where people had been dug up from their long rest. As for the joy my face showed, it was due to the love and friendship that my soul foresaw would unite us . . .

When a soul has been tuned by suffering, meditation and prayer, it will find unexpected power to overcome time and circumstances. For such a soul, faith becomes 'the substance of things hoped for', and love a flame which warms, enlivens and enlightens. With my earthly vision I looked in fear at the hundred or so women among whom I was to live. But in my soul a marvellous scenario was already unfolding in which the majority of these heroines, now powerless and unresisting in the face of suffering, would gain strength and courage. Marcella, Marie, Alexandra, Lydia, what spiritual riches lay hidden within you! And you, dear Gina – I still seem to see your bored expression as you made your way to the guard's side, when in reality my arrival had utterly shaken you . . . I can still hear your voice, harsh, cold, cutting.

'There are no beds available, Madam, but other people can share.'

She raised her voice to reach the women exercising in the courtyard: 'Who will share their beds with the newcomers?'

There was a long silence.

'Well, you can sort it out among yourselves,' said the warder.

'Come with me,' said Gina, the head of the 'section'. 'Put your stuff on the table.'

In the middle of the large room stood the table, with benches on either side. Apart from that there was nothing but row upon row of iron beds, stacked two or three together. At the far end of the room was a wash-basin, a big barrel, and the little door leading to the toilet.

As she explained the rules of our life together Gina refused to meet my eyes. Her movements and words revealed a sort of nervous tension and clumsiness. Covertly I observed her gentle, distinguished features, her ash-blond hair and her green eyes. Her gracious manner and the way she held her head, slightly tilted to the right, gave her an air of unquestionable elegance not masked by the depressing furnishings or the dress of striped homespun.

'That's fine,' I said. 'I'll get used to it. I'm really happy to be with you all: I've been alone in a cell since I was first arrested . . .'

Gina interrupted my friendly little speech. She didn't seem to have heard a word.

'I'll ask Cathy to share her bed with you,' she added, and went to call Cathy in from outside.

The girl accepted the idea with a good grace. I thanked them both, but added,

'Why can't I sleep on the floor? There's no need to disturb Cathy.'

'You're not allowed to sleep on the floor. As for disturbing her,' Gina smiled ironically. 'Maybe Cathy will be disturbing you. She's got an open sore all the way down her leg. It's not very pleasant when you're under the same blanket . . . Now, go and find your bed.'

Cathy took my hand and led me across to the end of the room. The last bed in the first row, one cage among the rest, would be my lair.

'Don't worry about it,' said Cathy encouragingly. 'I won't touch you with my bad leg. We'll get along, the two of us . . . What's your name?'

'Nicole.'

'It's a pretty name.' She paused. 'Nicole, don't think badly of Gina. She's a bit difficult, because she's very unhappy, more than the rest of us. I'll tell you everything I know . . .'

Exercise over, my comrades filed indoors again. The warder slammed the door and turned the keys roughly. When her footsteps had died away, my new companions rushed to crowd round my 'home'. Questions came at me from all sides, while curious, inquisitive eyes stared at me. I got the impression that some of my answers seemed to reassure these women, shut away for two years, as they learnt the most recent political news.

'Five months ago,' I told them, 'the provisional governments of the occupied countries made a concerted protest against the massive wave of arrests. The representative of the White House had been to Moscow to try and get those in prison released. The countries of the West are constantly putting on pressure to the same end. The radio and the press are full of it. There are demonstrations everywhere: hundreds of thousands of people in the streets demanding that political prisoners should be released. Diplomats are insisting that there must be free elections in all the countries held by the Soviets. The Americans are threatening the Soviets too. If the free elections and a general amnesty do not take place, they will stop all commercial traffic. Not to mention the new atomic weapon which is frightening Moscow . . .'

Later that night I was sorry for the things I had told them: was it right to encourage these women with human actions and promises, instead of pointing them towards the Lord? Salvation comes from Him alone. But I grew happier as I listened to their restless, disturbed sleep. 'Ultimately,' I consoled myself, 'well-intentioned words at the right moment can surely do no harm.'

* * *

Next morning Cathy woke me gently. She gave me a string of useful hints which henceforth would be a part of my daily routine. As the morning's early bustle died away a ghastly silence fell upon the dormitory. For the most part the women were lost in their own thoughts, staring into space. A few gossipped quietly.

'Cathy, why are they so silent?'

'That's prison regulations.'

'But there are no prison staff here to stop people talking, moving, smiling . . .'

'The warder's at her desk outside. And Gina insists on silence too.'

'Gina . . .'

'Ah, yes! Come closer, I'll tell you about her. Gina arrived in prison a week after her husband. It was like this: they had been divorced, but they still lived in the same house. Gina had a friend, a former minister. As he was being sought by the police he asked Gina to hide him in her flat, where he stayed for some months, with the connivance of Gina's ex-husband. But their son, a lad of fifteen, told everything to one of his friends to show his parents' courage. The police got wind of the matter (how, that's another story) and some days later they surrounded Gina's house. The friend jumped from the window and was cut down by the police. Gina's husband was arrested at once, and they took her in the following week.'

'That's terrible . . . what about the boy?'

'Wait, you'll see. Some time later, after Gina had been interrogated, she was taken by a Black Maria to this prison. There were several men in the van, and she asked them whether, by chance, any of them had met a man called Eugene Bratin in prison. One of the prisoners informed her that he had left him just an hour before, and that Bratin was in a state of despair because someone who had recently joined them had told him that his son had committed suicide. The boy had not been able to stand the weight on his conscience. You understand? The poor fellow was telling Gina all the details of the matter without realising that she was one of the victims of the tragedy. Gina arrived in a state of shock. She threw herself on her bed and wept without ceasing. We just didn't know how to comfort her. We wept with her. When Marcelle got here, the woman over there sitting by the window, she was very moved to discover Gina, as they had apparently known one another since childhood. Marcelle, who knew all about the affair, denied categorically that Michel, Gina's son, had committed suicide. She insisted that he was alive, that he was perfectly well and that the information Gina had received must have been invented by the police to demoralise her. As a result, Gina has grown more and more upset ever since. She resents Marcelle and won't speak to her for long periods; or will wake her in the middle of the night to beg her to tell her everything. As for Marcelle, she continues to hide the truth. She thought that a lie would calm Gina, but the reverse has happened. Now that she's no longer sure what the real truth is, she has grown more and more miserable and reserved. She's afraid every time a new prisoner arrives, because she may know something of the truth. But I think that Gina doesn't want to know any longer: she shrinks away and gets harder and harder, but still she clings to a vestige of hope that Marcelle may have told the truth.'

Some women who seemed to belong to the 'central committee' in the cell came across to question us in detail about a variety of matters: our ages, professions and in particular our political affiliations.

Marie de Layo didn't stand for this treatment very long, replying that such things were for the police to discover. Her bold, original, amusing manner soon allowed her to carve herself a comfortable niche among a number of others who belonged to no political party, but had worked before or during the war in the police department, the censor's office or on some democratic paper.

I had nothing to hide, so I told them that I was a member of the National People's Party, for whom I had worked, secretly during the war and openly from 1944 onwards until it was suppressed by the government of the day, already Communist-controlled. I did not know that Mislea had been opened once again as a prison on May 15th, 1948 for a group belonging to the extreme right who in 1949 still formed a considerable majority of the prisoners there. I quickly saw that for the moment I was the only one present representing my party. That was why that night, and many following, I was required to share my bed with Cathy. I have to admit that it was not pleasant to help with the poor girl's bandages. The unhappy creature would uncover her sore, pour on a liquid from the infirmary and replace the bandage, first reversing it. Each day I watched her apply this treatment, and each night shared her bed, keenly aware that my political aspirations were responsible for my particular lot.

Nobody had wanted to know Cathy since her sore had opened up, and she was grateful that I had accepted a place in her bed so willingly. She would not let me straighten the covers, and taking no notice of my protests did every one of my daily tasks (newcomers were required to empty the latrines, wash the floor, fetch the water, etc.)

Marie de Layo, however, refused to perform any chores, raising her voice and demonstrating that she had a stiff ankle because of the blows that she had received during questioning. From then on, no matter what, she would accept no work at all.

When I tried to stop Cathy working in my stead, she argued that she also performed such services for others, who used to pass her cigarettes for doing their tasks.

'But I've got nothing to give you.'

'I don't want anything. I like you, because you share a bed with me.'

She humped one burden after another right through the

day: rubbish, water, food . . . I was not sure whether in my weakened state I should have been able to summon up such efforts.

During the exercise hour, however, Cathy got her reward. As soon as we got into the courtyard, she tiptoed up to me and asked, 'Would you like to walk with me?'

'Why not, if we're allowed to.'

'I'd like to go arm in arm with you so that all the girls and the warders can see that I'm walking with a girl-friend.'

'But Cathy, don't you ever walk with anyone?'

'No, no one. Cathy is only good for work. I've never had a friend, or someone to share my bed at Mislea. They all think so much of themselves.'

I too was happy to walk with Cathy, as apart from her no one had spoken to me. It stayed that way for days.

This contact with the women imprisoned at Mislea seems to me, over all, to have been the most important experience of my life. Living with people so different socially, politically, and intellectually, together with the isolation which the majority imposed on me, all these elements had their effect, carving in me a bitter furrow of suffering.

* * *

Time passed, and the cell filled up. A tense atmosphere developed when Elena Codreanu and Iridenta Mota arrived, respectively the wife and sister of Corneliu Codreanu, who had been assassinated as the head of the rightist Iron Guard movement: they were followed by Marie Antonescu, wife of Marshal Antonescu who as an ally of Hitler had governed the country during the war years. The 'legionaries' (the name given to the members of the Iron Guard) gathered in groups: some belonged to the 'Codreanu' group, without however accepting Elena; others chose Iridenta, still others Elena Patrascu, wife of the legionary who had established a non-aggression pact with the Communists, only to find himself well and truly trapped by his agreement. A further section supported Horia Sima, who had fled the country, or Mironovici, a legionary of some standing who did not see eye to eye with any of the others. But despite these divisions, the stamp of their class and education was evident in these women from the start. They kept their opinions to themselves, did not argue even if they had different ideas, closed ranks to face difficulties, did not use threats to each other, and did not complain about each other. What was more, despite the utter poverty in the prison each package a legionary received was shared between them all, taking no notice of the differences between them.

In the meantime I was striking up a sort of friendship with a teacher from a small Moldavian village. Her bed was directly above ours. She suffered from tuberculosis, and was incapable of washing the dormitory floor when her turn came round. The last parcel her husband had sent her contained cigarettes, but she had received no parcels for months, and she feared that he too might have been arrested.

I took my place in the life of the *lagher*, carrying out my duties like the rest. As Cathy did not wish to go on washing and slaving for our neighbour, I took her place. Sandrine, poor girl, did not know how she could thank me, and I only managed to placate her when I explained, using her vocabulary, that I was 'offering up' my labours for my sins.

'Ah, that's good. I can see that you're offering plenty for your sins, even if only by doing your chores. Are you sure you're not working a bit too hard?'

'Don't worry about that. I'm glad to do it.'

So I found there was someone else I could get close to. She was very much alone, and constantly turned things over and over in her mind, creating worries for herself. What if they had arrested her husband, what about their possessions, few as they were? If they had tortured him during the questioning, she would be involved in a trial of some kind; whereas if on the other hand he remained free, sooner or later they would acknowledge she was innocent.

I did my best to persuade her that everything depended on the One who is Lord of our life on this earth, and that instead of tormenting herself it would be more to the point to ask His help.

'Do you think I'm some kind of pagan? I never go to bed without crossing myself, and I say the "Our Father" each morning. But everything in its season: just because I believe in God it doesn't mean that I'm not going to expect the justice owed me by men. They did me wrong, it's up to them to see me right.'

'If it's God's will,' I would repeat after each such argument.

In the long run a rift developed between us. Sandrine frequently avoided me. I was well aware of what she needed: a real faith. I prayed for her, as indeed for all the women we were living with.

Cathy seemed to understand me better and better, and this encouraged her for several days at a stretch to unfold 'the story of her life', full of the so-called errors of youth. Cathy realised that she was a sinner as she brought to light memories she had forgotten, and managed to see herself as she truly was, in all the smallness and confusion of her wanderings from the straight and narrow. Then she felt the need to pray. As it was impossible for us to pray together, I taught her what to say to Jesus at night, when all was quiet. And Cathy prayed. She would stay awake, I sensed, and sometimes I felt her crying. Afterwards, probably after she had prayed, she would turn towards me and kiss me on the forehead.

The joy that came to me during those nights is beyond words. Cathy had changed out of all recognition in the two weeks since she had started to pray.

Christmas drew near. One day Cathy climbed up on a bench in the middle of the room and shouted:

'Attention! Attention! This is to let you know that I'm available to help anyone who doesn't have the strength to work, and you can forget the cigarettes!'

'All right,' commented several voices, 'what are you asking in payment?'

'Nothing. All gratis and done with a smile.'

CHAPTER THREE

In the meantime a fearful enemy had appeared on the horizon: hunger.

The amount of food we received was not enough to satisfy us. Most of the other women received parcels every month – sometimes less frequently, depending on the whim of the prison officers and also on their families' means. They therefore usually had at least a little sugar, a biscuit or a small piece of bacon. I used to wake up so hungry that I would imagine someone above me was eating fresh croissants, as crusty as a French baguette: I could hear the golden crust crunching between their teeth . . . In reality it was nothing more than the bed creaking as Sandrine turned over.

Apart from my obsessive physical hunger, I was acutely aware of the need for someone with whom I could develop a spiritual link, someone among my companions in suffering with whom I could talk. I needed a deep friendship, which I was unable to find – until the day our director paid us a surprise visit one morning. She was accompanied by the chief warder, the chief woman warder, the prison doctor and the hospital orderly.

Although we were in a communal cell we had to make our beds when the prison 'opened', that is, at six in the morning, and then sit either on our beds or on the benches next to the table in the centre until the evening, when the prison 'closed'.

We could hear the director's voice in the yard outside the enclosure, giving us all time to straighten our sheets, which had to be arranged with the utmost precision, as in the army. Everyone fussed round her bed, trying to make it as presentable as possible, and darting frightened glances about. The director was known as a particularly strict woman, even cruel; she would lash out, curse, criticise sarcastically. I was taken aback, however, by the terror revealed in most of the faces around me, especially the legionaries'.

The door opened, and we jumped to our feet. The director was carrying some blank postcards.

Everyone snapped to attention. 'At your service!' they shouted.

The director's glance swept round the room. She began to criticise, lacing her speech with obscenities, pointing to the floor, which she considered dirty, and the beds, which were not sufficiently regular for her taste; she bawled everything at the top of her voice.

Then she called for the most recent arrivals. There were five of us: the women I have mentioned above, Marie de Layo and myself.

'Why were you arrested?'

'The enquiry revealed that I had been an imperialist spy.'

'And what about you?'

'I was arrested on August 24th. I was questioned about my part in the National People's Party during the Nazi oppression and after, up until the party was banned.'

'So you're a tzarist?'*

'The fact that I'm here proves it. If I had abandoned my opinions there'd have been no reason to arrest me!'

'So you stick to your ideas, even though you've been brought here for re-education?'

'I'm well aware that I need re-educating, but only in the negative aspects of my character, not in the areas where I know I am innocent, and where I have been able to

* In Rumania this meant a member of the National People's Party.

appreciate in the calm of my cell that I was right to act as I did.'

'You really believe that the National People's Party was engaged in a just and honest campaign, though it was the party of the bourgeoisie which exploited and crushed the majority of our country's people, the peasants?'

'I have decided that everything created by the hands and minds of men is imperfect. In comparison with other movements, however, I reckon that the National People's Party was the one which most benefited the peasants.'

'So you also believed in that dolt Maniu, that pervert and womaniser? I knew him personally. I was commanded to infiltrate the party secretly so as to pass back to the Communists everything which had a bearing on the doctrines and actions of the tzarists. So, my dear, I too have been a tzarist!' She burst out laughing at her own witticism. 'Yes, I knew Maniu personally. He was a fancy-boy, soft, always in opposition. He cloaked himself with a sort of legend which had been cooked up by his followers.'

I let her talk, waiting completely calmly. When she had finished, delighted at having humiliated one human being and insulted another, I replied:

'Madam director, I am sorry to have to remind you that I am a political prisoner and that this requires me to have the courage of my convictions. As a member of a political party and a Communist, you can have the worst possible opinion of my party, and express it openly. But as I am a prisoner solely on account of my political activities, allow me to say that it is one thing not to share a political opinion, and even to oppose it, as in your case, but that to insult a movement and its leader seems to me both unjust and graceless, especially in a prison with ninety per cent political prisoners. If we are here it's because of our opinions. I do not consider that I am here to change my opinions, and replace them by others, but purely and simply so as not to block the development of the party currently in power. Must we also suffer humiliation for our political opinions? We are already paying dearly for our past. I am not speaking for myself, but because of what you have said about Iuliu Maniu. He was no idiot, but rather an old man, and he had the courage to refuse to flee to the West for safety, in spite of his age. He insisted on staying in his country among those who belonged to his movement, whom he did not wish to betray and to whom he had sacrificed his whole life. But if his point of view does not agree with yours, at least he should receive the respect due to an old man who today is in prison because of his ideas.'

That was more or less my reply. I spoke gently and softly, so that they would let me finish what I had to say. The director's staring eyes and tense air indicated that my punishment would certainly be severe.

To my immense surprise and to our general astonishment, when I had finished my speech the director was silent for several moments. Her stance relaxed, and in a carefully controlled voice, which echoed strangely in the room's deathly silence, she said:

'Come over here. Closer. Is that your bed at the end?'

'Yes, madam director.'

'Who do you sleep with?'

'Cathy.'

'Ah, yes, the Hungarian girl.' She glanced around the room with a mocking smile. As I came forward, she added, 'Come on, dear, come right up. Tell me once again that you're one of Maniu's tzarists.'

'Yes, madam.'

'And you dare to tell me that, though I'm a Communist and a prison director, and to cap it all, you dare to criticise the way I choose to express myself?'

'I wasn't trying to teach you anything, madam. I only wished to defend, as I should, a worthy man and a patriot. I took up his defence, witn every respect, because it was my duty, no matter what the risk.'

She hesitated for long seconds. Then she beckoned me with a wide sweep of her hand.

'Closer!'

I moved forward slowly, sensing she was going to strike me.

As I approached, my eyes on hers, I did not glance aside to see the terrified faces of my companions. When I reached her, she said:

'Turn round and face the dormitory.' Then she added, addressing the prisoners, 'Did you hear how you ought to speak, how someone speaks when they're a real human being? She didn't mumble, "I don't know why they arrested me . . . it's all a mistake . . . they mixed up the names . . . I don't know . . . I haven't done anything . . ."'

She turned back to me.

'I first visited the *lagher* in May, 1948. Since then I have provoked every single prisoner to see whether a few at least would keep their dignity. I've insulted them, I've beaten them, I've threatened them with death, hoping that they would wake up and that one at least would react in a way worth respecting. In a word, that they would take a stand. "Why are you here?" I would ask them again and again. The reply was always the same: "I don't know," they whined. I have cursed your martyrs, I have insulted their memory, but no one has stood up to me. That's why I have never felt as though I was among political prisoners, and that's why I despised you. I still despise you . . .'

She nodded at me.

'I agree, you're a political prisoner, and you're in a prison for political prisoners, but I warn you to watch what you're saying: not everyone in charge has studied sociology and psychology like me . . .' Sitting on the table, one foot on the bench and hands on hips, she watched me with amusement. It was only then that I stiffened, feeling a kind of fear from within overwhelm me. I was just beginning to appreciate how strange the director's attitude was.

'Now, my dear, what have you done with your life so far?'

'Not all that much, madam. I'm hoping to redress the balance from now on . . .'

'Are you hoping to make tzarists of them all? Don't play with fire!'

'No, madam, that's not what I had in mind. Since I feel I can speak to you perfectly honestly, I can tell you I left my politics at the prison gate. Everything has its season. When I was in solitary confinement I was able to understand that there are causes in life which call for complete self-sacrifice, and the only banner worth following is Christianity. I'm an Orthodox believer. I was converted before my arrest, and since then I have decided to consecrate all my energy while I'm still young to Jesus, the Lord of all. He is the One I want to serve, and through Him, to serve those around me. My politics brought me here, but they no longer have any influence on me. I believe I'm a new creature as a result of my faith in God.'

'You're talking nonsense,' she commented, but in a much milder voice. 'Well, then the Communists brought you here: when can we start re-educating you?'

'You told me yourself, madam, re-education comes through hard work and discipline. On that level I'm prepared to obey without arguing. But nothing in the world is going to change what I believe inside.'

Another silence stretched endlessly. At last the director rose, her expression hardening.

'Bah! The legionaries also claim to believe in God. But as soon as I've gone you'll see exactly what their beliefs mean. Look at their faces: look at the hatred on them. How they'd avenge themselves if they had the chance! The beatings I got at their headquarters in the Rue Roma would be nothing by comparison with the tortures they'd subject me to if the wheel was to put them at the top once more . . .'

She swung round on one of the oldest prisoners. 'Right, Pica Bârlea?'

'Not in the least, madam,' the other replied timidly.

'Can you hear her lying?' she asked me. She turned back to Pica. 'Lying! and I've got the courage to tell you so. I can understand you, it's perfectly normal for you to hate me, given our different positions. The fact is that you can do nothing to me now, but you're dreaming of revenge and that warms your heart. Oh yes, I understand you. But what would really please me would be for you to say it to my face. Show me how you hate me. Admit it!'

Pica Bârlea was silent, a miserable expression on her face. I grasped my courage with both hands and answered the director myself.

'Madam, suffering can make you a finer person. When your heart has been broken, hatred and vengeance have no place in it. Here each one of us is tested. We are all the more capable of tolerating and forgiving those who treat us unjustly or punish us, as in this case. We can't assess whether we are guilty as far as those who run the country, and therefore our own rulers, are concerned, but only in relation to God. If we have sinned, it's Him we have displeased. Why should a woman like Pica Bârlea hate you? She's a Christian. She's able to love you, it's one of the main aims of Christianity, but in no way is she going to hate you or take revenge on you.'

The director's tone was scornful. 'It's up to you. I couldn't give a damn about your hatred. I've other things to worry about, and I've also got a revolver and the key to your "paradise". I'm sick of the lot of you!'

Cathy found the courage to speak up in her stumbling Rumanian.

'Madam, Pica is very good, and so is Nicole. I am sure that Nicole will pray for madam, really.'

'Get lost, pig! I don't need anyone's prayers. I pray to Lenin and Stalin: they're my gods.'

She abruptly held out the postcards to me. As she turned to go she flung a final instruction over her shoulder:

'The newcomers can share them out!'

She stamped out with her escort, leaving the atmosphere charged. After they had left there was silence for some moments. My forehead ran with sweat. I felt exhausted, as if I had worked myself to the limit. Everyone stood rooted to the spot. The only sounds were boots pacing and the creak of padlocks. The director's voice could no longer be heard.

Suddenly the tension broke. Spontaneously they surrounded me, hugged me, clustered close and pressed around me; congratulations showered on me from all corners of the dormitory. It was the first time that my fellow-prisoners had shown any warmth towards me: now, without exception, they stood round me with tears in their eyes, telling me how afraid they had been for me during my dialogue with the director and how much they had admired my words.

'You don't understand the risk you were taking. You don't know what that viper's capable of. She could tear out your eyes and beat you black and blue. She's a monster.'

'She attacks us for not acknowledging our political leanings and for failing to adopt a position. But who should we adopt a position for? For a pest of a woman who would profit from any confidence on our part and make our lives even harder?'

'I don't think you have to adopt any sort of political position. But as far as I'm concerned I've got nothing to hide.'

As I spoke a wave of exhaustion overcame me. I had opened my mouth without realising what I was doing, as if someone had taken control of me.

'You were great! It was fantastic! God protected you. Your faith saved you!'

In fact I had not wanted a confrontation with the director, and had not really been aware of what I was undertaking. As I was speaking I realised the danger, but I let myself be carried along as if by a torrent. From hearsay I knew of the director's cruelty, and from my own experience I was well aware of the rigours of Communist prisons. But a boldness and an exhilaration stronger than all such reasonings made me speak out all the same.

The first, and highly positive, result of my audacity was to shatter at a stroke the ice which separated me from my companions. As the first wave of emotion died away we became still closer, as if by a miracle. A strong bond began to develop between us.

Did I need this closeness? Yes, without a doubt, but above all I was sure that everyone else would profit by it. This first drawing together was one result: I was still obsessed with the spiritual vocation of sharing with others the joy within me. From my corner at the end of the dormitory I had seen and heard a good deal: some were on the verge of despair, others had lost hope altogether, and all felt crushed by the prison and by their concern for their families.

Anna, for example, was the mother of four children. Her father, a famous general, had been deported to Russia, as had her husband, and she knew that her children were alone in the house. Her three girls were between twelve and fifteen years old: there was a little lad even younger. Anna never moved, but thought constantly of her family. She would avoid all company, react to nothing, speak to nobody. She was always distant, far away: during the exercise hour she preferred to stay stretched on her bed. After the episode with the director, however, from time to time she would gratify me with a warm glance in my direction.

One day I resolved to talk to her. Briefly she told me about her tragedy and her fears that the State might place her children in a home and have them educated under the Communist system. She sobbed softly, mourning for her children, alone and helpless.

I told her that God would not leave poor innocent children to the mercy of fate. She leapt up as though she had been burnt.

'For heaven's sake, spare me that rubbish. If God exists, why does He allow this kind of cruelty against my family and other people? If God existed the best thing He could do would be to let me go home to look after my children!'

Piecing together Anna's words and the snatches of conversation I had had with most of the women in the dormitory, I realised that they had only the flimsiest basis for their Christian faith and their hope in God.

Communist regimes find it easy to destroy, morally and physically, those who are not prepared for real suffering. Day after day they eat away the soul, sometimes through terrifying interrogations, sometimes through sheer exhaustion, sometimes by imposing impossible work targets in forced labour camps – and also by depriving prisoners of all forms of intellectual expression (total absence of information and a ban on reading). In this way the Communists succeed in deadening both mind and intelligence, while because of the injustice many have experienced they lose their faith or hurl terrible accusations at God.

* * *

During this period at Mislea the prisoners were still allowed to receive a food parcel each month weighing five kilos. Those among my companions who had belonged to the Iron Guard used to remove a portion of each parcel, placing it in a cloth bag which they would throw through the bars of the enclosure next door when we took our exercise. Next door the rations were almost always reduced to a quarter of the normal level. This 'operation' was very risky, and could only be carried out when the warders were busy with something else and not watching the manoeuvre.

One glorious day there was a parcel for me in the consignment. This moved me more than words can say. It was true that we did not receive the parcels as they had been despatched, and so could not tell how they had been put together: otherwise it would have been possible to imagine, recognise and love the movements of those we held dear: but after an earlier inspection at the main office we were given the different foodstuffs all mingled together in a pillow-case or a piece of cloth. Sometimes washing powder would be mixed with sugar, and the bacon with the biscuits . . . All the same, it brought us untold joy. Such unforgettable moments drew us close to our dear ones and made us feel we were breathing the very air of our distant homes.

My first parcel contained something more precious than all the rest. They had overlooked a box of aspirin (like all other forms of medicine it should have been deposited at the infirmary, where in case of need you could ask for it in small doses). I was happier still when I found on the side of the box the word 'aspirin' in three different handwritings: my father's, my mother's, and my brother's. Poor loves! They had each written the word so that I would know that they were alive and free . . . That little word held real magic for me, full of new strength. Someone more experienced than they had probably told them to write something or other wherever it was possible, but only the box of aspirin had reached me. What a gift from God! I wept for joy as I looked at that little box. I kept it for a long time.

Then I quietly went about dividing the parcel under Cathy's starving gaze (she never received anything: her family lived in Hungary). Cathy and Sandrine, of course, were the special guests at this first feast. That evening I invited them to 'sit down to table'. As a tablecloth I spread a scarf, also from the parcel, across my bed (after my talk with the director the woman in charge of the dormitory had assigned me a bed of my own). Then, much later, when most of the dormitory was sleeping, I sought out Gina, the dormitory leader, and gave her half the good things I had received, packed into a little bag sewn specially for the purpose. I asked her to throw it through the bars of the neighbouring enclosure as circumstances allowed.

'What are you doing that for?' she asked. 'First, that's far too much, and in any case you know that there are only legionaries over there: I think you realise that there isn't a single tzarist . . .'

'Of course I know. What's the difference? They're hungry, and that's all I care about.'

'Yes, I understand, but all the same . . .'

'Please, take it and don't mention it in the dormitory. If I had your experience I would throw it by myself, but at the moment I don't know enough. That's why I'm asking you.'

'Thanks for everything.'

'I'm the one who should thank you for the joy you've given me.'

'God bless you, Nicole.'

I went to bed happy. Firstly because of the 'news' from home, then because of the gift I'd given, but also because I felt closer to Gina, who had smiled tenderly at me. She was all the dearer to me because of the deep misery within her.

* * *

I tried to sleep, but in vain. The image of my family haunted me. My thoughts were in a whirl. How much had that parcel cost them? They had gone without bread they needed just to spoil me. Perhaps they had saved up for five kilos of provisions by scrimping on their own food. How difficult it must have been to get them . . . Hot tears ran down my cheeks and I buried my face in my pillow. After some time I realised that I was wallowing in my own misery. Shaking myself as if coming out of a nightmare I prayed to God to give me my earlier calm and balance, so that I could use my time in prison to the utmost, particularly as I had already been able to reach several women in the dormitory. They were becoming my friends, for the most part, but as yet I had not managed to speak of God to them as I should do: I hadn't the skill. I was too much of a sinner to give them lessons! What could I say about sin! I had sinned more myself than many of them. If I couldn't speak to them in words, I would have to speak through my behaviour all the more; I would have to reflect God's presence, so as to make them want to learn the secret of my peace and joy in the face of adversity.

The day after my nocturnal conversation with Gina, we felt closer to one another. There was a complicity, in the best sense of the word, which linked us together. Nevertheless we exchanged not a syllable: I knew she would do what was necessary.

That afternoon, during the exercise period, Gina came over to me. She respected my wish to keep the matter secret.

'So I can throw the food, I've got hold of four little bags which can go through the bars. Try to talk with the warder while I'm busy.'

Taking Cathy with me I walked across to the guard to distract her from what was happening by the windows of the enclosure. I began to talk fervently about the dry ground around the plane tree, the only scrap of vegetation in our little yard. The warder, who had been there when I had confronted the director, had dubbed me a 'manist'* and treated me well enough, apart from the odd attack, which was understandable in a person as simple and miserable as she was.

To gain time I suggested that in the spring she might bring some seeds so that we could grow flowers in our drab yard.

'So you're asking for flowers now! Don't count on it: I've got to stick to the rules. It's not a hotel here, it's a prison.'

'I know it's a prison, madam, but think of us – nothing to see but smoke-blackened walls! A few flowers would add colour. Do you know what a flower would mean to us in our present misery? When you leave the prison, you at least can enjoy the sight of grass and trees.'

'Do you really think I see anything? When I'm here the whole day in prison with you? When I get back, I've got to cook supper for the children, feed the poultry . . . believe me, I've got no time to spend looking at things. Time and again I've had to go to sleep fully clothed at midnight, only to be up once more at four in the morning!'

'Yes, you really do have a hard life. But at least you're free . . .'

'Yes, free to work myself into the ground. You get food and exercise. By comparison, I'm worse off.'

'That's easy to say . . . but God save you from such food and such exercise!'

'And what's more, I've got a sore place between my toes and on my feet. It's running and it smells bad, and it's

* A follower of Iuliu Maniu.

simply the result of wearing boots all the time. I've not even had the time to go and see a doctor. Do you know, sometimes I even sleep with my boots on, because if I took them off it would stink out the whole house!'

'Perhaps it's an infection brought on by the sweat. You ought to see a doctor, especially if it's smelling.'

As I chatted with the guard I stole glances over her shoulder at Gina, who had matters well under way and had managed to pass three bags across.

Suddenly there was a noise from that direction. The last bag would not go through the bars and fell heavily on to the stone under the window.

The guard instinctively seized her weapon, thinking that one of the prisoners had tried to jump the wall. She whirled round towards the noise, catching Gina with the bag in her hand. She was in the middle of a fresh attempt to thrust the package through the bars.

'Stay right where you are!' shouted the guard. 'Don't move!'

Several prisoners gathered to watch what was going on. Others pretended to have noticed nothing and to know nothing about it. It's always better to know nothing.

'Give me that bag. What's in it?'

Gina held it out to her. She knew only too well what was in store: the bag would be confiscated, then there would be an enquiry at the office, and perhaps even a spell in the pound for herself.

The guard peered into the bag. 'Ah, so you're passing food to the ones being punished,' she commented. 'So . . .' She raised her voice to shout to the whole yard. 'Everyone in the dormitory, quick! Everyone inside! As for you, Bratin, stay with me, we're going to see the director.'

I went over to the guard. 'Madam, please let me explain. Bratin isn't guilty, I am. I gave her the bag and asked her to throw it into the pound. The food in the bag came from my parcel. I could only enjoy it if I was able to share it. I insisted that Bratin should throw it over. So I'm the one you should be taking to the director, it's me you should be punishing.'

Gina broke in. 'The food came from her, but I agreed to push it through the bars. Let's go together.'

'No, madam, I should be going alone. I'm the only one who's guilty.'

'I can see you want to come. You know that you've got a fine tongue in your head and that you're going to spin the director a yarn like last time, when my feet were sweating just at the thought of what was in store for you after what you said! Right, you can come, but she's coming too. Perhaps your fine phrases will do for both of you!'

'Madam, it's not just a question of us two. Think of the women shut away in there for no reason at all. The director may punish them too, though they're suffering enough already. How could they know someone would be passing them that little bag? Couldn't you let us both off this time? It won't happen again.'

'Let you off? Just so that one of the women in the pound can tell on me for not reporting you? So that I can find myself in with you for nothing? Not a hope.'

'Who would tell on you, madam? There's no one like that among us.'

'That's what you think. I shall say no more. Come on, both of you, with the bag and the rest of it.'

Somehow I had the boldness to try once more. 'Madam, we understand that for your own peace of mind you must file a report. But as it's my fault, as I practically forced Bratin to throw the bag, let me take all the consequences. I can promise you that no one will say anything different. Hardly anyone saw what happened. The others were exercising and then you bundled them all into the dormitory.'

The guard seemed less sure of herself. In a milder tone of voice, she commented,

'Look, if you're the only one who's guilty, what's Bratin doing with us outside?'

'Easy! She's in charge of the dormitory. You kept her

back to sort the situation out. Oh please, just take me, you'll see that that's the best way.'

'But . . . you want me to say that I didn't see her throwing the bag?'

'What does it matter who threw it? The important thing is who started it.'

Feeling that she was on the point of giving in, I added emphatically,

'In political trials, the instigator is the one who's considered guilty.'

Gina tried to break in, wanting to come with me, but I cut her off and drowned what she was saying.

'Just take me. I'm the guilty one. The director can punish me as she likes. I'm the one who's guilty, and I'm ready to take my punishment. Bratin is ill and she's been in prison longer . . .'

I was ready to come out with my strongest argument, Gina's constant misery, but I didn't need to. The guard seemed to understand what was going to happen, and said with an understanding smile,

'Right, as you like . . . come on then, come with me by yourself.'

Gina, far from happy, shot a reproachful glance at me. But I took her hand and squeezed it hard, looking at her warmly.

The guard sent her into the dormitory, closed the doors one after the other, then with her revolver trained on me, urged me out into the main yard.

For a moment I turned my head towards the building and saw a host of faces at the high windows. A number of women perched on the top beds were following me with their eyes. I naturally smiled at them, but could make no other gesture. The guard had recovered her dignity and the air of cruelty she had dropped for a few minutes. On the way to the director's office, she told me,

'Watch out, don't forget! You're the one who tried to throw the bag. Don't tell it any other way.'

'Don't worry. In any case, that's the truth: I'm the one

behind the whole affair.'

All hell had broken loose in the director's office. She was dressing down the woman in charge of the workshops. As she saw me, escorted by the guard, she broke off her shouting to snap,

'What's happened?'

'Excuse me, Comrade Commandant. During the exercise period they were trying to pass this package of food through into the pound.'

I would not let her go any further, but spoke up for everyone to hear.

'I wanted to get it through to the women in isolation, but the guard here saw me. She sent all the women back into the dormitory and brought me along to you. I realise I have broken the prison rules and I am ready to accept whatever punishment you wish to give me.'

'What's in the bag?' asked the director, anxious to get back to her argument with the workshop manageress.

'Food from the parcel I got yesterday,' I told her.

'Do you mean that you wanted to share your parcel with the women in the enclosure?'

'Yes, I thought that as they did not get any I would like to give them a little happiness.'

'Make that scum happy?'

I kept silent.

'Admit that you wanted to help that scum.'

I felt transfixed by her steely eyes. She turned to the guard.

'Note the following. One, the prisoner is to receive no parcels for the next month. Two, parcels are to be returned to the sender with the information that they will only be able to send three-kilo parcels instead of five.' She turned back to face me.

'You don't need more than that, since you give the rest away . . . and now, since you don't need extra food and since you're so bold, you can go over to the depot until it closes to move the boxes and sacks which have arrived from Ploesti. Then you'll be taken to the cooler to remind you that you're in prison and not in some kind of charitable institution, and that you've got to obey the rules. Get on with it!'

The guard led me off to the depot.

CHAPTER FOUR

The largest yard of the former monastery, now our prison, was overlooked by what had once been a church. Now, deconsecrated, it was used as a depot. All sorts of goods were stacked there for the kitchen and the workshops. The three guards who kept watch over the ordinary prisoners seemed to have a certain rapport with them. One looked after the church, another stood in front of the door to the kitchen and the third faced the workshops.

My guard left me in their tender care.

'Put yourself over there between those two big girls, they'll help you lift the boxes and bundles,' said one. She motioned to the fat women. 'Watch yourselves, we are honoured with the presence of a lady amongst us, a "political". Show her what you can do!'

As I entered the church my feelings were so strong that none of their rough gibes affected me. I bent, not only to pick up a box, but more especially to show respect, to acknowledge where I was. For a few seconds I was far away, then I felt able to lift a box to my shoulder, though with a terrible struggle. The fat women had already grasped their burdens, and I took my place among the laggards. They laughed so much at me that they seemed almost possessed.

'Well, ducks, it's hard to work like a slave when you're a lady!'

'You should have been good to the poor if you didn't want to find yourself here!'

'Your hands are really soft, aren't they?'

'What's it like to have a box on your shoulder instead of a fine fur coat?'

Not replying to their jests, I went on with my work as best I could. I looked forward impatiently to getting back to the church, and I prayed non-stop. That quietened the women. They realised that their gibes were having no effect on me.

All of a sudden the order was given to stop shifting boxes and instead to take bundles over to the workshops. I couldn't even lift one, let alone carry it on my shoulder. With immense difficulty I wrestled it up into my arms. As I bent to pick it up, however, I suddenly noticed to my right a number of religious objects behind the bundles – a candle, a mitre and two books, one of which had to be a large Bible. My first thought was to grab it and run! 'How can I get hold of it?' I thought. 'Oh, Lord, give us this Bible!'

On the way from the church to the workshops and back I formulated my plan. I undid the buttons on my skirt, keeping it up with my elbows. As I got to the book I seized it furtively, thrust it up into the front of my blouse and did myself up again. No one saw anything: I was still the last in the task-force. As I lifted each bundle I adjusted my prize better until I was sure it would not slip.

I was highly excited, and my joy brought a flush to my cheeks and neck. I felt utterly exhausted.

'The "lady's" ready to drop,' said one of the guards.

'Sit down for a bit,' said a prisoner.

'No, no, it's all right, thanks,' I said, not wanting to stay in one place lest I draw attention to my over-ample bosom.

'Go ahead, if you want to die, the cemetery's behind the church. All the same, I'm going to warn your guard: you look as though you're about to catch fire.'

She called 'my' guard over, and they whispered together for a few minutes. Meanwhile I went on with my work, praying constantly.

'Hey, you! Come on, you've worked enough. It's a quarter to six. I'll take you to your new apartment. No more work or boxes there. You'll be standing the whole night, that cell is tiny, just what's needed for tall ladies who are worried about their figures.' She cackled.

Putting down the last bundle, I pretended to be hollow-chested. It was true in a sense: I felt quite wrung out, and great drops of sweat were running down my face.

The guards said goodbye to each other, and mine told me, 'Whose fault is it? You shouldn't try to be good. It'll be tough in the cell, but I'll bring you some water.'

'Thanks, no, don't worry about me. But I thank you from the bottom of my heart for your kind thought. God won't forget.'

'Drop the God bit, will you? If He existed He wouldn't have let you get caught when you were trying to help others!'

A surge of joy rushed through me. 'Who knows why He let me be caught? No one can know what God is planning . . .'

'Stay right there with your God, then,' she retorted as she opened the cell door. 'I hope I find you alive tomorrow morning.'

Relief washed over me as I heard her footsteps die away. The tiredness, the pains, the bowed back vanished.

The book had a thick cardboard cover. I hardly had room to use my arms, but in the end I managed to tear it off. I placed the cover at my back, separate from the book, between my shirt and my prison uniform. The book I held in my hands, stroking it. I was confident that my tight skirt would not let my beautiful prize slip. I eagerly anticipated the next day: my companions would discover the Holy Scriptures!

When I returned to my cell next morning I received a warm welcome. My friends gathered round me, happy to find me safe and sound. By some means or another I was given a big cup of hot sweet tea, and answered a good number of questions on my stay in the 'cooler'. When calm had descended again and everyone had gone about their business, I clambered up on to one of the top bunks and announced:

'Yesterday's adventure has had one extraordinary result. I've come back from the cooler with the most important book in the world – the Bible!'

As I explained the details of my theft, I undid my blouse and showed them the incredible booty which had resulted from my punishment.

'Do you agree we should keep this Bible here and read it? It's a majority decision. If you vote 'yes', raise your right hands. I promise I'll take all responsibility if it's discovered.'

Every hand went up spontaneously, except for Marie de Layo's. She commented, 'I don't agree, because I don't believe and I don't see what use this book could have. But I promise I'll keep my mouth shut.'

* * *

So that everyone could get the maximum advantage from our Bible, we set about splitting it up into sixty-six books of the Old and New Testaments. Each book was then sewn into cloth covers to strengthen it.

Everything was fine, except for one point: it was impossible to finish reading a book because another started on the same page. This wasn't serious, as the sixty-six books passed constantly from hand to hand, and from soul to soul.

Our little holy library, in an old metal biscuit box, was hidden away each evening and whenever a search threatened, secreted in the old water cistern for the dormitory's toilets, which had not worked for a long time.

For years this improvised library worked miracles by God's grace. During the two years I spent in that prison I witnessed many a moving conversion, cries of sorrow and joy, profound changes in character, new life springing up.

How long did that Bible continue its ministry of resurrection among the prisoners there? The woman who told me about it, and who had been blessed by reading it, had just completed a six-year sentence. Therefore, four years after I had been transferred to hard labour the Bible was still circulating among the prisoners of Mislea, spreading its message of light and truth to the depths of anguished souls, and strengthening the faith of those nearer God.

As I remember that morning when I returned in triumph with our Bible, I can still hear the discussions that followed. Apart from Marie de Layo, who didn't want us to keep and read it, the others for the most part were happy to have something to read, and what a book!

After I had drunk my tea and recovered somewhat from my churning emotions and weariness, I was called on to answer a host of questions. In the monotony of our daily lives, such a matter deserved to be analysed, appreciated in every detail. I found myself on Gina's bed, opposite mine but one level higher, so I could answer the questions that came at me more easily. I was so delighted to draw closer to my companions, and especially to Gina, who held my hand and was stroking it, that I failed to notice Marie de Layo and a group of five or six others looking at me in scorn. One might have thought that Marie was only waiting for me to get my breath back before she intervened.

She broke in with carefully calculated spontaneity.

'Listen, dear, spare us your stories, I've had enough of your delusions of grandeur: offering half your parcel to the legionaries, taking the blame for someone else, accepting punishment, stealing the Bible! What's all the fuss about? Perhaps you want to make your mark with the legionaries, so that you can turn it to advantage when they come to power again? They've had their chance, you know!'

'I wasn't thinking of that,' I told her. 'You've got it completely wrong. And I don't even want to answer you when you accuse me of that sort of calculation.'

The whole dormitory was on edge. No one wanted to poison the atmosphere. Then Cathy leapt in.

'Shut up, de Layo. You're bad, but this lady is good, very good. You see how good she is, and that makes you sad, because you are wicked and quarrelsome, and no one likes you!'

'Oh, yes, she's good!' she replied, more to the room at large than to Cathy. 'I know all about good people. They're everything you could wish for, *except* good. Perhaps she can pass herself off as a good woman, but the most she can do is to try to become one. That's what I think, and I'm never wrong in my judgments!'

I raised my voice to carry above the disapproving murmurs which arose on all sides.

'You're right, Marie de Layo. You're right: I don't feel at all good. But I try to be, and I'm still hoping that one day I really shall be. I know that God let me be sent to prison so that He could raise my soul from the depths and transform my evil nature. I'm sure that He has the power to change me. Maybe I'll never reach the goodness the Gospel speaks of; human life is too short to reach such perfection. But at least my soul will be comforted by the presence of goodness, even if it is not very strong within me. Without being too modest, I know that there is some good in me, but not in any depth. I can see when I should be standing up for the truth, just as practically speaking I can observe the results of wickedness, and I'm glad. Since I know the difference, and since I want what is right, I've already been able to do some good. But I can only really hope to improve through perseverence – and prayer.'

'You see? I was right!' she crowed. 'I saw just what she was worth.'

'Yes, you're right, de Layo, and I'm grateful to you for helping me to admit something as serious as this in public. It was probably necessary . . . after what happened yesterday, and the warm way our friends received me this morning, their admiration might have made me think too highly of myself. I might have got all puffed up for no reason. But thanks to you, I can see everything in its proper perspective. Many thanks.'

'Isn't she amazing?' she asked the room as a whole. 'A woman just like me, and she's getting God to make her perfect!'

'Yes, of course. God made good use of the ravens to feed Elijah. There are many ways He can change our hearts.'

'Well, don't let Him try them on me, because I'll send Him packing double quick!'

I didn't reply. The others rose to shut her up.

* * *

From the day the Bible started circulating among us, our life together changed direction. The separate books of the Bible – we called them booklets – were too few for each person to read them individually. We therefore set up reading groups: from Genesis to Revelation, the pages of holy scripture passed from hand to hand, and practically everyone had the chance to see them.

When we had finished our tasks each morning, we ate our breakfast (a dish of boiled maize called *tertch*), and an air of calm would fall upon the dormitory. When I was still finding my feet after my arrival I had already noticed this sudden calm, but now it was different: it was shared. Previously, women used to lie on their bunks for hours on end, staring at the ceiling or the walls; others hissed bitter words at one another or built castles in their imagination for the day when they would be released; some, exhausted, lay passively on the lower beds. Now, however, groups would gather to read with reverence from the book which had been brought into the cell so marvellously, and which we kept at such risk.

We were constantly aware of the guards' movements. As soon as the key was heard in the padlock we would thrust the books under the mattresses, the women adopting their previous pose of indifference, or pretending to spin some yarn. The days passed calmly and swiftly, faster than before. Some stood watch, because apart from the guard you could always expect a surprise visit from the director. In that case we had to rush everything back into the box, which would then be safely hidden. I often took this responsibility on myself, to allow the others to read in peace: in any case, I was the one who looked after the box.

They would come to me each morning.

'Here's Matthew back. What've you got free?'

'The Psalms.'

'Fine, but please let me have Mark when it's available.'

At first they read the books merely for pleasure, non-stop like a novel. But a point came when the Bible had passed through each person's hands and soul at least once. I was overjoyed to see how the women would then often interrupt their reading to discuss the passages that seemed most important or the hardest to understand. The Epistles received the most attention, because the majority of the women had gone through the Gospels at school, during the years when teaching was still free of political strictures and religion was a subject like any other. The Epistles made a strong impact on everyone. Sometimes those studying the Old Testament would hear others reading one of the Epistles, and break off to start a discussion together. Certain passages in the Old Testament were harder. But what interested the women above all was the way the ideas in the Epistles could be applied in daily life.

So that we shouldn't forget the Old Testament, however – as more and more were studying the Epistles – we introduced a different system. In the morning we would read in tighter groups, always taking care that the overall appearance of the dormitory remained unchanged, because the guard could come in at any moment. We also made sure that nothing could be heard outside. First of all would come a portion of the New Testament, with a commentary, and then the group would read from the different books as before. Studying in larger groups gave rise to a range of thoughts. Everyone had to say what she understood from the passage, and in this way whole pages could grow clear.

One day I suggested, 'Do you think we ought to read a psalm together, to make our sharing a bit more solemn? We could start with Psalm 1. We could do this with the whole dormitory, especially where the shorter psalms are concerned.'

We did as I had suggested for a week.

The following Sunday the church bells in the village

seemed to ring more loudly than before. One of the women had an idea.

'Today's Sunday! Shouldn't we start our reading with a prayer? Who's going to pray?'

Marcella said the Lord's Prayer, then Lucia recited the Creed.

That morning affected us deeply. During the two prayers, many sighed, while others wept softly. There was a long silence. Then, as if someone had waved a magic wand the women began to kiss and hug one another. Only Marie de Layo's group held itself aloof from our fellowship. We remained standing for a few minutes, motionless. When we had dried our tears, we found ourselves a little embarrassed by our emotions and did not know quite what to say. The smallest word, in any case, would have broken the spell.

One thing alone prevented us from basking fully in the light which our reading of the Bible cast upon us, with our interpretation of its pages: this was the constant watch we had to keep on the guards' movements. We also had to maintain unceasing vigilance not to be caught out by a surprise visit from our director, and found it galling to read with our voices hushed at all times. We needed to exercise extreme care in our discussions. Instead of complaining, however, we had only praise and thanks for the One who allowed us to enjoy His presence among us through His Word, which constantly warmed our souls. As we assimilated page after wonderful page, and understood them more and more fully, each day we grew closer to God.

* * *

One afternoon, during our exercise period, Gina came across to me and we walked a little way together.

'I wanted you to know,' she told me, 'that though I feel guilty about a lot of different sins, the one that lies heaviest on my conscience is the fact that I've had abortion after abortion. From the moment I started reading the Bible, I felt – I knew – that I had sinned before God in preventing human beings from being born to live on this earth. I have gone against God's plans . . . I have thought a lot about my own tragedy, which I'm sure you know: if it is true that my child has died a shameful death, I'm the one who must bear the responsibility. Do you think I will be forgiven one day?'

'I believe that if someone knows they sinned, if they repent and believe in the redeeming power of the Saviour's blood, then they are forgiven.'

'But how can I right the wrong I have done?'

'At the moment you are suffering, and that will help to wipe it out. Then you can move to a higher level; you can start to act constructively, spiritually speaking, and begin to repair the damage.'

'Do you believe I'll be able to have another child?'

'Why not? In any case, we don't know how God works. Perhaps you can repair the evil you've done in another way – in a quite different realm, not by having another child.'

'I pray all the time. I don't know how to pray, but I list all the things which weigh upon my mind like a sort of complaint, and that's what I'm calling prayer.'

'And afterwards, don't you feel any easier?'

'Yes, indeed. Sometimes. But I know you've got to persevere. Will you pray for me too?'

'I've been doing that for a long time.'

We embraced each other.

CHAPTER FIVE

Spring had come. The buds were breaking on the tree in our yard. As nature came to life, it generated in us a kind of impatience, the desire to escape, a thirst for liberty.

Easter drew near, making us all the more conscious of how we missed those dear to us. Sundays and the prospect of major festivals usually made us long more acutely for those who were far away.

There were more and more women in the cell. Recent arrivals had included an Orthodox nun, Mother Eudoxie. She was Moldavian, and spoke softly and gently. She comforted us a great deal.

Each Sunday Mother Eudoxie would begin our improvised service with a prayer. The poor woman had been arrested for sheltering fugitives. She had had no idea who they were, nor why they were on the run. They were caught, and denounced her as the one who had hidden them, thus succeeding in concealing the identity of others who had taken them in. Mother Eudoxie, however, bore not the slightest grudge against them, but rather prayed for them and for their freedom.

The presence of so many newcomers required us to use our 'library' more carefully. We old-timers managed to gather together so that our beds formed a compact group where we could be close to one another. Then when we were sure that one of the others was reliable, we would let her in on our secret. In this way a number joined us.

To celebrate Easter, we decided first of all to read from the Way of the Cross during Holy Week, and to think deeply about the sufferings of Jesus. His final prayer was very dear to me. Many had learnt it by heart: many, in fact, had got into the habit of learning whole pages of the Bible. We were storing food in case of bad times to come, for we were sure that one day we would leave the prison. Where would we be going? No one knew. Our departure was imminent, however: according to the newcomers and the rumours which circulated through the prison, the State was in the process of building a canal which would link the Danube to the Black Sea somewhere in Dobroudja, and they were sending hundreds of thousands of men for forced labour. It seemed that in the near future the women too would have to go.

I was extremely sad at the thought of being separated from my sisters in prison. The only thing which could lift that shadow, which fell upon my soul when I thought of our impending separation, was the idea that I could be of use to others elsewhere. What God had done at Mislea could happen again at the canal. I was in any case at His disposal, and I did not allow such gloomy thoughts to find a place in my heart.

Those of us who had followed the Way of the Cross decided to hold a vigil during the night before Easter Sunday. We would wake at midnight and in silence celebrate the resurrection with our own service.

When the bells rang in the village, more than fifty of us were standing by our beds. Mother Eudoxie, who was leading us, sat on one of the upper beds, so that everyone could hear the whispered readings and prayers.

After the resurrection bells had chimed and when Mother Eudoxie had read us the appropriate passages in each of the gospels, we shared the traditional greeting: 'Christ is risen!', to which we replied together: 'He is risen, He is risen indeed!'

At the risk of being heard (though we had closed all the windows), we burst forth together into the wonderful

Orthodox chant 'Christ is risen from the dead', repeating it three times as is the custom. The whole dormitory awoke. The moment was so solemn and such joy filled the air, that nearly everyone climbed down from their beds to join their voices with ours. If the guard had been at her post, she would certainly have heard us, but at night the watch was maintained outside the second courtyard which separated the prison from the offices and the infirmary. In any case, a light burned all night in the dormitory, which reassured the warder that nothing untoward was happening.

We stood for several minutes, softly chanting the same holy words to different tunes. A sense of peace stole through the whole dormitory, shared by all apart from a few Jewesses, and, of course, Marie de Layo, who pretended to be asleep. When the bells in the little village church had fallen silent, we repeated 'Christ is risen' to one another and returned to our beds. As we opened the windows again a breeze, heavy with spring scents, crept into the room. Far though we were from those we loved, forced to live in foul conditions, we were nevertheless closer to God. We appreciated more fully the mystery of the resurrection than when we had celebrated Easter at liberty. Now we understood its marvellous beauty.

That Easter night gave rise to a custom. We decided to form a chain of prayer which would start at five in the morning and finish at midnight with worship together. During the day, each person would pray silently for ten minutes: this required real concentration because of the constant hum of voices in the dormitory. At midnight, when a siren would sound some way off (Mislea was near the richest oil-bearing region of Rumania), the woman who formed the last link in the chain would wake us all. We silently got out of bed. The space available was narrow and there were a good many of us, and this crowding together brought us still closer for our nocturnal prayer. The circle of prayer grew and grew, including two Jewesses who had told us they wished to 'pray to their God' with us. Each soul that joined us gave cause for fresh rejoicing, and so we prayed together. The theme of our prayers changed constantly: one day it would be for our families, then for those in our dormitory, or in the other enclosure, or for the whole prison, for those in every prison, for the salvation of the souls of those who were our masters, for the liberation of our whole country . . . these hours of praise together did wonderful things for us, crowning the work that God's Word had done as it sank into each of our minds. It was a completely natural act, a need felt by a host of souls united together in one faith and hope.

* * *

One morning, one of the ordinary prisoners who brought us the cauldrons of food took the opportunity to whisper to Gina, who with the warder was responsible for distributing the *tertch*. 'War has broken out in Corinth,' she muttered. Once the can was empty and the door shut, Gina passed on the news to us.

'What did she say? Are you sure it's really war? Why Corinth?'

Questions rained on Gina, who was growing increasingly excited, as was everyone else.

'If it's Corinth, that means that the Americans have landed and are going to overrun Europe.'

'See, they haven't abandoned us! From Corinth they'll go on up through Yugoslavia, and from there they'll get through into Rumania!'

'You reckon the Russians will let themselves be had so easily? They're bound to stick their oar in!'

'She said that war had broken out at Corinth, she didn't say, "The Americans have landed there", but it's war for certain.'

'You're right, Nina, it is war. But if the Americans *are* at Corinth, that means that the Russians aren't putting up much resistance.'

'What's more, the Americans aren't going to turn up with their hands in their pockets. When you think of their unbeatable air force . . . and as they will have mobilised all their resources, they're going to crush the Russians to powder.'

There was a tremendous commotion in the dormitory. The warder intervened several times, but without success. Some of the women were already looking at her in pity. We felt as though the Americans were already there, that they had reached the very gates of the prison.

Although we had advised discretion with regard to those in whom we did not have complete confidence, within a few minutes the whole dormitory had heard the news, and was in a state of feverish excitement. The guard stayed in the room to calm us down.

Each of us, whether on her bed or on the benches in the centre, had abandoned her prayers to weave wild dreams about freedom. A kind of hysterical optimism overwhelmed us. We were quite unable to control ourselves.

'What's got into you today?' screamed the warder.

'Nothing at all,' said de Layo. 'They're just in heat and they don't have any men.'

This crack amused the warder, and gave rise to an unseemly dialogue between her and Marie. They laughed together, making all kinds of allusions to our supposedly 'nervy' condition. Once again, as had often happened, Marie de Layo's intervention had saved us. However, their conversation now included indecent words and anecdotes in the same vein.

I realised how utterly superficial we were. The idea of freedom, the rumour that a war might release us from prison was stronger than all the faith which had developed within us during the many preceding months . . . We had forgotten our prayers, not feeling the least need of them. How strong the Tempter is! I shared this insight with Gina, and then with the rest. Even little Mother Eudoxie had been electrified by news of the war.

Withdrawing into myself, I sat down on the edge of my bed, trying to concentrate and regain control.

Then I turned towards Gina and the others and suggested that it was not wise to let ourselves be carried away by a mere rumour, and that even if liberation was only one step away, that was no reason to forget the daily duty which we had taken upon ourselves, the chain of prayer.

Gradually, people grew calmer.

All the same, right through the day they talked of nothing else. At lunch Gina asked the prisoner who brought the food if the rumour was still going round. She replied that it was not just a rumour, but a positive fact.

During the exercise period some of our number tried to get the news through to those in the pound. Others pulled themselves up to the windows to try and signal prisoners in the workshops; from time to time one of them would emerge to go from one workshop to another, thereby crossing the yard. We had a number of small dodges for getting in touch with them, but these were reserved for important occasions, as the risk was immense. That day, however, attempts to make contact went on constantly.

Magda, a highly experienced prisoner, who had also been imprisoned under previous regimes, asked to be taken over to the infirmary, claiming severe stomach pains. The warder led her out. When she returned, Magda told us that the woman in charge, an ordinary prisoner, had confirmed by signals the outbreak of war. What was more, she had seen the director walking agitatedly in the yard with two high-ranking military officers. The director had been talking non-stop and gesticulating vigorously.

'Listen,' said Mica, 'it's not out of the question that we could be deported or even killed. I reckon that's what will happen to us if the Americans don't find us.'

Her neighbour disagreed. 'Why should it be us at Mislea who get deported or killed? You really think that? They'll take care of the men first!'

'Bravo!' cut in de Layo suddenly. 'So that's your charity, you Christian saints. You're so happy that others are suffering. There's your brotherly love: let them slaughter the men, but not you.'

'You haven't understood a thing,' was the rejoinder.

'You never understand anything, and you're always sticking your nose into what doesn't concern you.'

Discussions continued right through the day. We were very troubled, and it was only with difficulty that we kept up the chain of prayer.

When the evening meal arrived the prisoner was questioned further and again she confirmed that the information was accurate. As soon as the door was locked everyone lay down. That evening there was no question of stories or conversation. No one even read the Bible. In any case, the box had stayed in its hiding place all day.

Some time later a tremendous uproar in the dormitory woke me suddenly. At first I did not understand what was happening. In the middle of the night a group of male and female warders had burst into the room, led by the director and two or three ranking officers from the Militia. The director was shouting at the top of her voice.

'Everyone up! In two minutes I want you dressed and lined up at the door! Move!'

We all concentrated on dressing as quickly as possible, thinking of nothing but the two minutes we had to put on our prison jackets and to form a line. The director went on shouting, using every kind of epithet. The strange officers pretended to study the ceiling and the walls. The warders were everywhere, their weapons trained on us as if we had been surprised in the middle of some unlawful deed or an escape attempt.

Finally, more or less two minutes later, everyone was ready. Raking our hair into place as we went, we moved forward in silence.

The door in the wall surrounding our little yard stood open. A weak light shone in the larger yard towards which we were driven, escorted by militiamen and our warders.

'Everyone against the wall!' rapped a man behind us. I realised we had got separated from our groups. One by one we made our way towards the three sides of the courtyard, and pressing close together we ranged ourselves against the brickwork. Once everyone was out and lined up the head warder shouted,

'Turn left to face the wall! Noses touching the wall. Move! No talking, look straight ahead!'

We obeyed. Our 'left wheel' rustled sinisterly in the still night. We could hear the warders and militiamen cocking the rifles they trained on us: they seemed about to fire.

We could no longer hear the director's voice. There was no way of knowing whether she was in the yard or the dormitory, or whether she had disappeared.

Noses against the wall, we were acutely aware of the weapons behind us. We expected the shooting to start at any moment. From time to time we could hear the owls which nested under the roof of our dormitory.

Suddenly, everything fell into place. The war in Corinth, the American invasion – they were going to gun us down as someone had suggested that morning. No time to lose! Quick, a last prayer –

'Lord, I put everything into Your hands. If You are letting me die now, forgive me for all my sins. Look upon me with pity. I am the least of Your creatures. Do not forget in Your mercy the love I hold for you. Forget my many wrongdoings. Be with those that I love. Strengthen those who share my suffering and all those who are to experience such moments and such emotions. Into Your hands I commend my spirit.'

All I could do now was wait. Out of the corner of my eye I could see the barrel of a sub-machine gun against the body of a woman nearby. I could almost hear my neighbours' hearts beating. From time to time the guards would move their weapons to check them. I waited for them to fire. After a while I began to wonder whether they had not already fired: perhaps I was already dead. It all seemed so unreal.

Suddenly Marie de Layo screamed, 'My child! He's going to lose his mother! You criminals!'

There was a flurry of blows from her direction, but Marie's cry had set off others. There was no shouting, rather sighs and weeping. The guards moved across, presumably towards those who were grieving.

'Quiet! Silence!'

No one breathed a word.

Death is preceded by such strange feelings. Having said one prayer, words failed me. I was a desert. I was waiting to make the great leap, to cross the threshold. I could call no face, no single memory to mind. I was utterly alone, face to face with death. On the other hand, I was aware that Jesus was there. I no longer heeded the sub-machine guns, nor the boots crunching as men walked back and forth across the yard. I felt there was nothing left to do. My life was totally in the past. People, movements, all had ceased to exist. I was separated from the world by an infinite gulf. If I remained aware of what was happening, it was simply to wait for the command to fire.

I thought . . . but how could I think since I no longer existed? The poor words I have will not let me tell it any other way . . . it was as though, my prayer ended, I had taken a sack containing my whole identity and cast it over the brink of a precipice, and now I stood on the edge myself. A moment later I would be leaping into the abyss, to find myself in Jesus' arms. All my fears had disappeared. I had no regrets, no hope of escaping. No thoughts, no 'why', no 'how', no reasoning, nothing whatsoever. I was not even aware of Jesus as I had been in my prayers. I had no concept or image of Him. He was the something, the everything into which I would sink in an instant.

As if in a dream, I heard the director shouting. It was dreadfully hard to come down to earth.

'Left turn! Move!'

Dawn was breaking. The director and the ranking officers were approaching from our dormitory, the strange soldiers bringing up the rear. The morning's light, still feeble, mingled with the yellowish glow from the lamp, tinting every face with a corpse-like pallor.

I was back in the world. As we obediently filed like robots towards the dormitory I tried to get a grip on myself.

I needed to recapture my soul, which had fled far away. I was still too numb to think or to draw conclusions. I was returning from death itself to what we call 'life'. One single perception overwhelmed me: life itself was indeed vanity. If Jesus were not there to love you and to wait for you, life would have no meaning whatsoever.

We poured pell-mell back into the dormitory. It looked as though a whirlwind had passed through the room. Gutted mattresses lay on the ground. Straw covered our belongings, our scraps of clothing, our nightshirts, all in utter disorder. The warders shouted,

'The search is over! Everything back in its place! Come on, get on with it!'

We stared at the sight like mad women, terrified. Our eyes still reflected the hours of fear we had lived through. No one had the slightest bitter comment for the way the search had been handled, nor the brutal indifference which had left the dormitory in such a state. We had returned from the dead. The thought that we had escaped dominated everything else. What did it matter if we had lost a few meagre supplies, or that it would take days to get things to rights? When the warder had closed and bolted the door, we stood petrified, our heads sunk on our chests. We had to make a superhuman effort to get a hold of ourselves. No one said a word. However, little by little, the first rays of the June sun revived us, and under the urging of Gina, who had regained her sang-froid, we scrabbled in the heap to remake our beds. Gina turned to me.

'The warders told me that we will be brought needles and thread to repair the damage.'

I looked at the women's faces. They seemed illumined by a calm light. There were no quarrels now as there had been once after a more minor search, when everyone had done her utmost to get hold of her own sheet or to find a toothbrush and the 'soap from home'. This time the shock had been too direct, too violent. No one had dared hope she might return to this dormitory alive.

Lenutza's voice sounded very far away.

‘What does it all mean? Did they go back on their decision to kill us? Perhaps they got orders at the last moment. Be with us, Holy Mother.’ She crossed herself three times.

Everyone had an opinion to express: they were all so grateful to be still alive.

Mother Eudoxie climbed up on a bench.

‘Come, dear friends, let us thank God for having saved us.’

I asked myself the point of this stormy night. Certainly, it had been a valuable lesson for each of us. A warning? A test? Perhaps a chance for some of us to make progress in our spiritual lives.

Pia and Zoë had already checked that our ‘library’ was safe in its hiding place. No one had thought of searching there.

Conversation ceased as the *tertch* was brought. Nobody asked the prisoner whether the war in Corinth had been confirmed. It no longer interested us. We had experienced too many strong emotions.

After the meal the prayer chain started up again as usual, but with much greater fervour. The ‘library’ was taken by storm.

Tears in her eyes, Anna came to confess, ‘I’ve done so much that was wrong. I didn’t believe God had any power. But if He protected me last night, as I dared to ask Him, then I’m sure He can look after my children too. From now on I’d like to join all you believers. But – please – arrange for a day of prayer for my children and for me.’

‘We just want you to join us. We’ve been praying for you and your children for a long time.’

The next night Anna was roused to take part in the chain of prayer.

* * *

The news of the search in our dormitory ran right through the prison. Our secret ‘antennae’ informed us that no one had slept that night. Everyone knew about the war in

Corinth and the American landings. The prisoners all expected that we would be the first victims and that in due course everyone else would suffer the same fate.

Some days after that memorable night Dorina, one of the political prisoners in the workshops, managed to tell Gina that war had indeed broken out – not in Corinth, but in Korea. Probably one of the ordinary prisoners, who like many others had access to the central offices, had cast her eyes over a paper and had said Corinth instead of Korea . . .

As for that terrible night, it transpired that it had been a spectacular search laid on by the director to demonstrate her strength and cruelty to the visiting inspectors.

What a superb lesson God had taught us! Each one of us profited by it according to her needs. Each person who had lived through that night had drawn on all her spiritual resources.

A host of events took place in that dormitory at Mislea. Our experiences ran the whole gamut, from tragedy to comedy, from wickedness to goodness, from despair to conversion – and by implication, the acquisition of an unshakeable hope.

I have seen in detail how different types of people react to situations. I've observed the effects of cowardice and dignity. I have met women in the grip of the Evil One, and I've seen people transformed by the Almighty.

But what I learned above all from those twenty months in the dormitory at Mislea is that God loves every one whom He has created, and that He desires them jealously for Himself. This is why He performed such wonders for us, the greatest of which was the provision of a Bible. Subsequently He called to Himself – through His Word, not through poor human ramblings – all those who would hear and respond to His summons. Even Anna, who had suffered in silence and would open her mouth only to insult the very idea of God, turned to Him.

When I was free I met Anna again. Her children had not found fosterparents, though every member of her family had been arrested. An aunt in Switzerland, who had decided to visit her family in Rumania, had discovered the little ones totally abandoned and had resolved to raise them herself until something else turned up.

As for Gina, she gained sufficient spiritual strength to face the terrible reality of her son's suicide. She was given the power to see things as they were, and to acknowledge the responsibility she shared for her child's irreparable gesture. She hoped that as she prayed and repented of all the evil in her past life, God would grant her His forgiveness.

There are many whom the Word of God has transformed to the depths of their being, sweeping away deep-rooted hates and political beliefs and revealing God's divine splendour in such a way that all earthly aspirations have faded, disappearing into the night.

There were many other events I cannot describe. Some matters are too personal to be revealed. Moreoever, I may not place at risk people still in the Communist world.

My thoughts and heart will always belong to those friends I hold so dear. Neither distance nor our brief separation can break those ties.

CHAPTER SIX

Mislea camp began to break up. Early in the autumn of 1951, women began to leave, ten at a time. No one knew where they were going, though we could be sure that they were not returning to their homes. We gathered that women were being transported to the canal to work alongside the men. This information confused us, since among those leaving were some who were seriously ill with heart trouble or tuberculosis. How could such women work? Perhaps it wasn't the canal . . .

Unrest was at a height. To meet all eventualities we exchanged addresses, giving each other commissions to fulfil in case one of us finally got home . . .

Our grief before such separations was terrible. The thought that we might be torn from one another made us all the more aware of our unity in the tightly-knit group we had formed. We loved one another like sisters. Each day we attempted to strengthen each other, wishing each other courage and strength, exhorting one another to hold fast to the hope that no matter what happened God would be with us. In this way we shared together the blessings of His love. We cared for those whose faith was weaker, passing on advice which would sustain them on the distant shores of the Black Sea. 'In any case,' we would say, 'who can tell? Maybe we'll meet each other there . . .'

Everyone agreed that the Bible should stay until the last person left. The last to leave Mislea should secure it in its hiding place, where it could stay in safety until someone discovered it. It was out of the question that it should fall into the administration's hands, after all the good it had done us. I was convinced that it would be saved for other prisoners.

One afternoon I heard someone call my name and five others. It was like a thunderbolt from a clear sky.

'Pick up all your stuff, and get moving!' said the warders.

They always used the same phrases, were always in a hurry, not even giving us time to embrace or shake hands. They watched us like women possessed, and if one of us whispered a word to a neighbour they showered threats and insults upon us.

I packed my bag. When I reached the door I turned to them all, my eyes full of tears, and called out,

'By God's grace we'll meet in freedom soon! I love you!'

The warder turned me roughly around and pushed me towards the corridor. I shall never forget the misery stamped on the faces I glimpsed as I went by.

She lined us up two by two, and before we crossed the yard she told us forcibly,

'No one's to turn towards the dormitory!'

We obeyed this order, but each of us sensed the gaze of those who remained behind, crowding to the high windows, until the great gate closed to hide us from their eyes.

The tribulations of our journey were only to be expected of the disordered bureaucracy and the regime's cruelty. We were bundled into a van and driven from Mislea to Ploesti. We waited about twelve hours in the town just before being taken to the station, where in a siding we were crammed into a coach with compartments, twelve of us for every six places. There were many more of us leaving Ploesti, as we had been joined by women from other prisons.

The journey to the canal lasted three days. Our coach formed part of all kinds of trains, making detours to different towns to pick up other prisoners who had been 'selected' to build the celebrated canal. We were each given a portion of cold food: bread, bacon, and stewed fruit. A kind of covered seat had been provided in the compartment for the calls of nature. However, it was quite a to-do to reach it, because it provided space for two people sitting jammed together.

* * *

It's hard to describe all the miseries of the journey: the quarrelling women, the recriminations, and in particular the lack of air and the cramped limbs which caused intense suffering for hours at a stretch. The six of us from Mislea were lost among the other occupants of the compartment. The windows were totally blocked by wood and iron bars. The only access to air was through a small space below the door into the corridor. The heat was stifling, and we were racked with thirst. We were only given small amounts of water at a time.

I was delighted when the women agreed to let me tell them of a similar journey made by the missionary Mathilda Wrede as she accompanied prisoners from Finland into Siberia. Among the seven women we did not know was the wife of the leader of the Jehovah's Witnesses. She told me she had read the book, and seemed happy to listen to me. When I described Mathilda Wrede, a pure and holy woman, who had rejected her rich family's life of luxury to give herself entirely to Christian work among criminals in Finnish prisons during the tzarist era, the women all forgot their uncomfortable positions and turned to face me. I was describing the suffering of certain prisoners being transported to Siberia in the depths of winter: the cold inside and outside the carriages, whose frozen doors would not close, the windows totally covered in ice, the scanty clothing – such details took our minds off our own sufferings. The women's curiosity reached its peak when they learned that Mathilda Wrede, on hearing of the convoy, managed to reach the point on the frontier where the road to Siberia started. Dressed like the prisoners in a flimsy blouse and without boots or clogs, she proved to the leader of the convoy that she had been specially authorised by the government to accompany the prisoners until they reached the camp of their destination.

'Why was she going with them too?'

'I thought they'd sentenced her as a missionary.'

'In those days,' I replied, 'it wasn't a crime to be a missionary, and Mathilda Wrede had a spiritual bond with many prisoners in that convoy, men whom she had often visited in prison and who in many cases had been converted.'

'Converts who had killed and stolen?' interjected a blonde girl with curly hair, who seemed an ordinary rather than a political prisoner.

'Of course. With a good deal of perseverence, Mathilda was able to show them that a man can be converted despite all the crimes he has committed, and that he too can obtain forgiveness by believing that our Saviour died on a cross for the sins of all men.'

'Like the thief who was crucified beside Jesus?'

'Exactly. In fact, that was the first argument Mathilda would use to those who acknowledged that they were guilty and were asking whether they deserved to be forgiven.'

'And they became Christians?'

'Yes indeed. And on this train there were many of these men, Mathilda's brothers in the faith. That's why she wanted to go with them. Although her health was poor she wished to share all their sufferings on that journey.'

'But they must have been particularly wicked to be sent to Siberia?' asked a prisoner whom I couldn't see, as she was hidden by a woman sitting on the lap of someone on the bench.

'Yes, they were well aware that because of their crimes they had to undergo years of punishment. Some had even been condemned to life imprisonment. But they accepted this earthly punishment because they knew they had been forgiven in the spirit. They were certain that when this life's sufferings were over they would enter eternity, where the Lord would view them not as criminals but as brothers.'

'You're talking as though someone had come back to tell

us what it's like,' objected an old woman with a seamed face and shifty eyes.

'Jesus himself came back,' replied Mia, who was one of my group.

'Rubbish!' commented another, 'but go on, keep talking. I like listening to your stories: they seem to come from another planet.'

I went on for as long as I could. Then Mia took over, as she too knew the story of Mathilda Wrede: I had told her in detail at Mislea.

Of course we could not fill out the whole journey with a single biography, no matter how marvellous. We tried to doze for a while. From time to time we had to move our limbs, a complicated business, as we were crushed together. Each person in turn would get to her feet to perform a few exercises, while the others shifted their legs a fraction to give her room. Several things sustained us: stories, sleep, such movements as were possible; above all the hope that the journey would come to an end. Several women fainted, but there was little we could do. The door to every compartment was blocked from the other side, as prisoners were even crowded into the corridor.

* * *

All of a sudden we found ourselves facing rows of barracks, stretching as far as the eye could see. The days of physical torment we had suffered were finally over.

We found it hard to stand up straight as we waited for the officer in charge to conduct the roll-call. The initial delay was long, but the roll-call lasted an eternity. The director of the women's camp, an important figure, seemed to have mastered the alphabet scarcely twenty-four hours previously. He went through real agonies as he spelt out our names and Christian names, and his dogged perseverance meant we were on our feet a good extra hour.

It is extraordinary to watch how people obey orders in Communist prisons. I simply do not know how the guards managed to make us disembark in silence, nor how they managed to conceal the many men on our train. As they shepherded the women out into a field to be counted, they succeeded in maintaining total order and calm. Did we fear the blows, or was it the insults which made us line up so efficiently and swiftly? At any rate, there was not the slightest sign of revolt or fatigue; not a single curse from the men. We must all have been model prisoners.

A woman told me once why she was always the last in line: to keep as far away as possible from the eye of the warders. 'I don't want to spark off any rows. I can't answer back to their filthy language, and I don't want to hear it. That's why I hang back so as not to attract their attention.'

When the formalities were finally completed, dawn was breaking. We left our 'luggage' at the store (keeping only the bare minimum, such as toothbrush, handkerchief and the clothes we stood up in) and were assembled in groups of four and bustled off towards the barracks.

The guards waited until the bell rang for reveille. Only then did we pass through the barbed wire to our new home. Before each barracks stood a woman in a striped top, watched by a warder, letting in a specific number of new arrivals depending on the places available in the dormitory.

One group of six was admitted to barracks Number Four, together with two other women. On the threshold we beheld a nightmarish scene.

On the beaten earth – there was no floor – stood two rows of wooden boards, each with a thin mattress and a sort of yellowish cloth which served as a sheet. The women, now roused, were rushing and scurrying to dress. In the midst of the mess a woman guard was shouting, 'Faster! Faster! They're going to call the roll!'

We could pick out no one person in the semi-darkness. The air was foul. The prisoners seemed highly agitated and had not even noticed our arrival. We stayed in a tight group, unable to mingle with these women who ran about like puppets.

The dormitory leader came in with her guard. Realising that we didn't know what to do next, she spoke kindly.

'Come with me, I'll show you your places.'

'Couldn't we have a corner just for the six of us?' asked Stella. 'We're all from the same prison.'

'I'll try. But I'll have to wait until the women have finished here and vacated their "four-posters". I can't do anything till then, if you're anxious to stay together. While you wait' – she moved over towards a table of rough timber – 'here are bowls and spoons.'

She looked down at our feet.

'I don't quite know what you can do about your shoes. We've only got heavy boots, but today you'll have to go as you are. There's a good deal of mud, but nothing we can do about it. Cope as best you can till this evening.'

'Is that because,' I began hesitantly, '. . . because we're leaving for work right away?'

'I'm afraid so.'

'But we haven't slept for three nights. We're stiff all over. We were squeezed into that compartment like sardines.'

'I know it only too well. I arrived here the same way. But my orders are to get you lined up with the rest of your dormitory at once.'

She saw the disillusion and weariness on our faces, and added:

'I'll try and find you a place in one of the political barracks. Where are you from? Mislea?'

'Yes,' we chorused.

'During the day, while you're at work, I'll try and arrange with the woman in charge of the political prisoners to get you a billet with them. There are lots of women from Mislea in the political section.'

'Mislea? From Mislea?'

'Certainly. Quite a number in fact, but they came one after another. Do you want to be put with them?'

'Please, if that's possible,' said Mia. 'That would be wonderful.'

'Right. Leave it to me. When you get back this evening, everything should be arranged. Now, go out and get your *tertch*. You'll discover that the discipline's very severe here.

If you don't knuckle under, the punishments are particularly hard: solitary confinement, beatings, reduced rations – greatly reduced. Considering how hard the work is, it's better to avoid that kind of "extra".'

We thanked her from the bottom of our hearts. She promised that she'd be with the other leaders that evening at the gate to show us to the barracks she'd mentioned. She very kindly gave us a small cloth bag each to hold our bowls and spoons, in the camp and at work. We would be brought our food on the job.

We were intrigued, but indecisive and off balance. As we talked with the leader the women were filing past us, bowl in hand, their bags over their shoulders. When we looked more closely in the full light of day, we saw that every woman wore large shoes covered in mud from the previous days, and in some cases straw protruded from them. To our cost we would discover a little later that shoes were not selected for style. As a rule you chose the largest, filling them with straw. You wallowed in the thickest mud: as the shoes did not fit, they would sink into it, and become exceedingly hard to withdraw. As you were afraid that the column would leave you behind, you dragged the shoe out with your hands and replaced it on a foot already plastered with mud. That wasn't the only problem to worry about: there was far worse to come. We were slaves in a forced labour camp.

* * *

As we went up, one after another, to receive our rations of *tertch*, our first impression was that no one had time for anyone. Life ran at a crazy pace in camp. Those in authority would tolerate nothing that broke up the rhythm of the day's work. We were taken aback at how impossible it was to stop and swap our different reactions: scarcely had we swallowed our *tertch* and stuffed our unwashed bowl and spoon into the bags than we had to line up by eights, to be pushed by the others towards the exit gate. As we looked around us we wondered whether we were dealing with civilised beings or savages. After the silence at Mislea the noise and chatter were incessant. Women quarrelled and talked; all you could hear were insults and foul jokes. On every subject and none, filthy words spattered the lips of the women in the column like mud.

'Mia, my little one! It's appalling! What have we fallen into?'

'Hell,' decided Stella.

We set off amidst the shouting women and the strident whistles of the guards, who seemed intent on driving us mad.

'How did the girls from Mislea stand it? Where are Paula, Pia, Maria Rotaru and the others? Is Paula still here in spite of her tuberculosis? Perhaps the politicals' dormitories are a bit cleaner, or perhaps the work's not so hard . . .'

Past the gate each rank of eight was duly counted. A host of militiamen surrounded us, their rifles at the ready. The three junior officers at the head of the column were very noisy, constantly blowing their whistles, but the guards on either side seemed quieter. We thought they found it as hard to drag themselves along as we did.

Near the exit the road was dry, but further on it bore signs of recent rain. The ground grew heavier, and heavier, softer and softer. It was hard for us to walk at the fairly rapid pace set by the head of the column. By ironic good luck our shoes stayed in place, as our feet had swollen during three days' forced inaction, and this stopped us from losing them. Some of those around us did lose a shoe, but merely cursed and set off again, wisecracking among themselves and even trying to joke with the guards, who pretended not to hear.

It wasn't hard to guess we were with ordinary prisoners. We did not strike up conversations with any of our neighbours. When we looked back, over the heads of the women, the column seemed endless. 'Where can the others be?' I wondered, and seethed with impatience to make contact with them on our return.

A few small villages and fields of clay bordered the road,

which as we learnt later was about four kilometres long: in this region the ground was poor. At the end we reached the 'restricted zone'. Armed soldiers in specially built observation towers toted sub-machine guns. There were four such towers, guarding the outer limits of the area in which we were forced to work.

Row after row left the long column and made their way to this area. When our turn came, we followed the others and among the general confusion, shouts and curses we jumped a ditch and reached our workplace. It was rocky, a huge pile of stones which from a distance seemed more like a small hill. Some way away were piled the tools cast down in disorder at the end of the previous day – picks, mattocks, shovels. We saw the women rushing at them, trampling on each other's feet, scrabbling for their instruments of torture. Subsequently I understood why: some of the tools were better than others, newer, keener; others were rusted, with too large a handle and therefore harder to use. The soldier called towards us:

'Hey! You over there! What are you waiting for? Get to work!'

'What should we do?'

'You'll say "sir" when you speak to me, get it? Now, get moving. You can see which tools are left, so take them.'

If only our families could have seen us! I and two others each had a wheelbarrow and a shovel. The rest had picks. The soldier stayed to guide us towards a knot of women who were starting work.

'You with the picks, get up the hill and the leaders there will tell you what to do. The ones with wheelbarrows will be shifting stones.'

The wheelbarrow was heavy, and was constantly refilled. By the time you had taken a quick breath and wiped your nose, it was already full. Then, overflowing with rocks, it had to be pushed a good hundred metres, crossing a ditch by a narrow plank on which you could scarcely keep your balance. You emptied it on the other side, and at once set out on the return journey without stopping for a single instant, teetering across another plank. The loaded barrows went one way, the empties another.

The wind suddenly picked up. I was cold because I was wearing little under my jacket. My mind was blank. The soldiers blew their whistles non-stop, goading us on. I had lost sight of my friends. The whole thing seemed a dream, a hallucination. The old-timers in the camp competed to see who could wield their picks best or push their barrows fastest, and I wondered where they got the strength. The wind, which was now gusting strongly, whipped up the dust and made it all the harder to cross the planks with the barrow. I could no longer keep my eyes open, I had to shield them from the dust.

All of a sudden there was a burst of lunatic shouting.

'It's here! It's here!'

A horse-drawn waggon appeared, a smaller one beside it. It was our meal and a supply of water.

It is hard to describe the racket and the growing excitement as the two carts approached. They stopped some distance away, and a soldier and the team leader moved towards them. A prolonged blast on the whistle apparently announced the lunch break.

The women flung themselves towards the casks like savages. It seemed the water was shared out first of all. In their haste to be first, they managed to spill a fair portion of it. Those who succeeded in getting some in their bowls gulped it straight down, then rushed towards the larger barrel. Here there was a little more order. A sort of queue formed up, each woman holding her bowl in her right hand as she passed the barrel, receiving a ladle full of something very liquid.

During the meal I joined the women from Mislea, the latest arrivals. We exchanged horrified, questioning glances, but said not a word (though we could talk freely). When we had received our food, we clustered round to see what it consisted of. In our bowls there was a yellowish liquid, odourless, almost as clear as water. It was cold. When we tried to raise our spoons to our mouths the strong wind spilled the liquid, flinging it over our clothes. I don't think any of us managed to swallow more than a few spoonfuls. A kind of yellow grease remained at the bottom of the empty bowl. We were surprised to see those who had finished eating heading back to the barrel to fill their bowls with water, but presumed that they intended to wash them. We learned later that they were keeping some water by for the afternoon, as no more would be brought to the site before work finished for the day. We would later understand a good many things we experienced that first day – and would behave just like the rest. At that moment however, we could not believe we would act this way.

Unfortunately such animal behaviour was to become second nature to us. During the months we worked on the canal we were forced to become as brutish as the rest, to work far beyond our natural strength, eat from unwashed bowls, and much more beside.

* * *

We were allowed little time for eating and relaxation. Thirty minutes later the whistles and shouts arose again. In the general pandemonium we bent to our task once more.

From time to time I stole a glance at the sky, hoping that evening might bring our first day of torment to a close. I had no idea what time it might be, and struggled on. At that moment I understood that in the case of many women here all physical resiliance would soon be completely wiped out.

After a while I caught sight of Mia, who was also pushing a barrow. She was extremely weak, and hollow-chested and suffered badly from rheumatism.

'I can't take any more!' she muttered.

Her words shook me. I was on the point of responding, 'Nor me,' but all of a sudden I remembered the cell at Malmaison Prison and the many hours of spiritual exaltation I had spent there. At the same time I recalled the decision that I had taken, never to let treacherous words such as, 'I can't stand it', 'I can't take it', pass my lips. I had become convinced that God never allows us to be tested beyond our strength if we trust in Him.

At once I felt a new strong confidence well up within my weary body. New power was flowing into me. I told Mia:

'*Never* say that. If you pray, God will give you all the strength you need to fight against tiredness and especially to keep your spirits up. When we're together this evening, we'll feel better and we'll be able to encourage one another.'

Over her shoulder, Mia smiled at me in gratitude.

Thinking positive and constructive thoughts, I lost all sense of time. I began to whistle the hymn I kept for bad days: 'My rock, my fortress, My shelter and protector, My succour in distress Is Jesus the Redeemer . . .' Mia took it up and unabashed we began to sing, without anyone stopping us. It was incredible to sing out loud like that. Till then, even at Mislea, we had only sung under our breath, but now the shouting around us gave us cover: no one heard us except for ourselves and God.

There came a point when we realised we could no longer hear even ourselves. A new wave of frenzied cries completely deafened us.

'Train! The train! There's the train!' howled the women, staring at the horizon. You could just make out a goods train with a string of oil containers.

We understood nothing of this, and merely took up our work again with new vigour. Perhaps thirty minutes later all the guards blew their whistles together; the women left their barrows where they were or flung their tools down where they had picked them up that morning, and piled over to the ditch separating us from the road, to start forming up in eights. Work was clearly over for the day. Inexperienced as we were, pushed and pulled in all directions, we were among the last to form up, but our group was together again. After the terrible day we were finally headed back to the barracks and rest – and above all, to our dear friends from Mislea.

* * *

The wind had dried the mud which helped our return, but it was hard to drag our poor swollen feet along.

Because of the dust, the sunset tinted the little clouds scattered here and there along the horizon with fantastic colours. The enchanting shades ranged from orange-red to pink, from blue to delicate mauve. We all stared at the sky. What a price we were paying, I thought, to enjoy this spectacle in all its various hues.

'But that's true,' I said to myself. 'You have to make a great deal of effort to achieve heavenly joy. I'll try and apply this to my daily life.'

We finally reached the gate, where we were counted just like sheep. We stopped beside our barracks in the yard to talk with the leaders of the dormitories. The head of our barracks came across.

'I have arranged with the camp administration to pass you over to the political barracks. Paula, Maria Rotaru and several others are waiting for you. Which of you is called Nicole?'

'Me.'

'Sabina sends her love.'

'Sabina? Which Sabina is that?' I asked myself. 'Could it be Sabina Wurmbrand?' Complex emotions went through my mind: joy at seeing her again, dismay that she should have been arrested and sent to this unbearable hole. The delay was equally unbearable. Could it really be Bintzea? It had to be, because I didn't know anyone else by that name. Then it hit me: the poor woman really was here, in this misery.

They kept us standing more than an hour in file, each block of eight waiting separately. Those to blame appeared later: the man who had spelt out our names when we first arrived, together with a number of others sporting the uniforms of high-ranking officers. It took them a long time to count us that evening, as the officers had the bad habit of setting down the numbers in a different fashion from the way we had been taught in school. They also forgot to put the single digits and the multiples of ten in different columns, and this always gave the wrong results, which could be astronomically high. However, they insisted on doing their sums themselves, though several dormitory leaders could have offered to help them. But that would only have annoyed them . . .

All in all it was quite dark before we were able to break ranks. At once we hurried to meet our leader, who with a warder led us to the barracks we were so anxious to reach.

A group of women was waiting on the threshold. We couldn't make out their faces in the distance, but as we got there our names were called and we found ourselves in their arms. Bintzea, the smallest, forced her way head first through the bodies blocking her path and we collapsed into each other's embrace.

Emotion overwhelmed us. Questions shot back and forth. Because of Bintzea I did not turn to the girls from Mislea – who knew, in any case, from past conversations of my friendship with her. They were well aware how much I loved her: later Bintzea told me that the group of legionaries who had learned of her through me were happy to make her welcome. This saved her from any anti-Jewish attacks (which did sometimes occur, especially when people were tired or under unusual strain): in fact the legionaries surrounded her with friendship and affection, loved her in their turn and considered her a pearl without price. Bintzea expounded the Old Testament to them: those who had read the Bible were thus able to refresh their memories, while those who had not been so fortunate heard passages from the Word of God, set forth as only Bintzea could.

* * *

I discovered that a year after my arrest the police had come to arrest her at the same house where I had been apprehended. She had no news of Richard, her husband, whom she loved dearly; there was even a rumour that he had died in Vacaresti, a prison in Bucharest. I had heard, however, from a woman passing through Mislea after her child had been born at Vacaresti, that in the hospital there was a pastor, tall but weak, who lost no opportunity to speak of salvation through Jesus Christ. I assured her that this could be none other than Richard and that he must be alive.

'How long ago was that?' asked Bintzea.

'1950. I'm pretty certain that he was taken to the hospital at Tîrgu-Ocna.' (The Ministry of the Interior had built a hospital there in the mountains for serious cases.)

'Do you think he would have got there, considering the conditions in which he must have been travelling?'

'Probably, really sick patients are carried differently. I know that at Vacaresti he was so ill that he was taken to the morgue because they thought he was going to die.'

'What if he did die there?'

'No, out of the question. Mona (the woman I'd met) saw him after that through a window, lying on a blanket in the yard. He was lifted with a number of others into an ambulance which was leaving for Tîrgu-Ocna.' I paused. 'Mona had no motive for lying to me. She didn't in the least suspect that I knew him when she described what she had seen. Apparently it moved the patients in the hospital at Vacaresti a good deal. She even believed that God had worked a remarkable miracle for the sake of a man who was utterly devoted to Him, because although he had been left in the morgue he survived to be transferred to somewhere healthier.'

'But you could tell he was ill?'

'Yes. He was very weak. His shirt was in tatters, she said, and he moved about with difficulty. But each time he crossed the ward he would stop at every door to say: "The Lord Jesus loves each one of you. Repent and you will be saved for all eternity. If any of you gets free some day, can he go and see my wife Sabina and my son Michael to tell them that I love them, but that I love God above all." Then he would give your address.'

'I've never had any news of him,' said Bintzea. 'I tried every way I knew.'

Arm in arm, we made our way into the dormitory. Here I was introduced to a number of other political prisoners hailing from every part of the country. They welcomed me surprisingly warmly. Everyone knew how we had lived at Mislea, and had been greatly encouraged by those who had discovered a keen new faith there, thus gaining strength to face the terrible human suffering on the canal.

Bintzea found me a place beside her. She would not let me go to fetch my evening meal, as she had prepared a special menu with the parcel she had been given in the visiting room.

As I talked with her I glanced across to where my friends from Mislea were sitting with other women working on the canal. To stop them thinking that I'd forgotten them or that I did not care for them so much, I broke off, went across to their trestle tables and told them, 'You know I love you all, but tonight Bintzea and I have so much to say to one another.'

'Don't worry about it, we're celebrating today.'

I hadn't noticed that each evening a group of ten women were called out for some sort of chore. Bintzea gave me details of the exhausting schedule of chores and commissions, a whole system designed to squeeze us dry, like lemons, before sending us on.

Bintzea was able to give me more recent news of my family. She had seen them the day before she was arrested. I was delighted to learn that my father was now receiving a pension (he had not been getting one when I left). A new law had made him eligible, and this at least gave my parents a basic income. Household expenses were covered by my mother's German lessons and piano lessons. Bintzea added that they went to church regularly and to the meeting there, and that above all they were longing to see me again. My brother was still a violinist with the Georges Enesco Philharmonic Orchestra, but lived in daily fear of being arrested again. Alice had taken in Michael, Sabina's son, and another boy the Wurmbrands were looking after, and was doing her best to bring them up. A good many faces that I loved drifted through the conversation that night. Sadly we were so tired that sleep overtook us as we talked.

* * *

The next day each of us bore her cross as best she might. The newcomers learnt from the old-timers how to eke out their efforts ounce by ounce so as to conserve their strength for as long as possible. As the political prisoners kept together we enjoyed greater quiet and order and mutual respect. However, the soldiers guarded us closely, burdening us with all kinds of useless tasks. We did them. At least we were not in the hellish conditions that had prevailed during our first day's work. We were together and we got on well. If one was too weak, the others helped her, so that the target we had been set was reached by the group as a whole.

The only moment of real relaxation was on Sunday afternoon between three and five, when we were left in peace. We worked through Saturday without a break, and on Sunday morning we would be allotted the most fatuous tasks – for example, turning over boundary stones so that they lay the other way up – no matter what, provided it prevented us from resting.

That first Sunday afternoon I got to know all the women in our political section, the girls, the older women and a large number of religious, both Catholic and Greek Orthodox. These last slept at the far end of the dormitory and prayed together constantly. They were generally liked and respected. Even the guards treated them with a kind of condescension, but this did not exempt them from the hardest and dirtiest jobs in the camp, nor from working side by side with the others. However, their faces radiated calm, and they worked well, even too well.

One of the people who made a particular impression on me was Sister Judith, who is now in America. She was then eighteen, and had been brought up by the nuns. Small-boned, delicate, pretty, with large gentle blue eyes, she was purity itself. They said she was consumptive.

After two months of non-stop backbreaking labour, we

were posted elsewhere. New orders had come through for us.

Our sections began to break up. They had been composed equally of political prisoners and common criminals, all the way from pick-pockets and prostitutes to the worst kinds of malefactor. We moved on from stone-shifting to building dykes, and then to digging holes for fruit-trees. The holes were a metre deep and a metre wide, and we had to complete eight each day. Sister Judith, whom we loved so much, could take no more, and fell ill. However, as she did not have the 'regulation' temperature of 38° at six a.m., she was not allowed to stay in barracks or go to the sick room. She was therefore ordered to take water out to the prisoners as they worked. The dykes, like the holes for the trees, were being prepared over considerable areas, and the ground was very uneven. The water wagon with its barrel would have been shaken about so much that it would all have been spilt by the time it got to us, so Sister Judith was assigned a bucket and a bowl to carry water from one prisoner to the next.

Although the ordinary prisoners in our ranks caused us a good deal of trouble, we managed to keep them in hand right to the end, except for a few recalcitrant individuals who would swear at us for no reason. The soldiers would support them, encouraging them to persecute and denounce us.

'They're all ladies from the days of the bourgeoisie,' they would call. 'It's their crimes that have made you become prostitutes and steal and kill!'

(I would love to know why there is a larger percentage of thieves, criminals and prostitutes in Rumania today, after the bourgeoisie has been destroyed and after thirty years of Communism.)

'Go ahead, don't be afraid!' the soldiers would jeer. 'Call them what you like. They're only getting what they deserve!'

We let them rattle on. Our common suffering strengthened us. We arranged that each time we were working with

Bintzea she would tell us a story from the Old Testament. Thus over a period of several months she told us the life of Joseph. Bintzea could really bring her narrative to life with her soothing voice, and she succeeded in establishing a strong link between Joseph's world and our own, the events of long ago and our lives today. We arranged it so that we could dig her holes for her. During checks she would pretend to wield a pick, but in fact we were all working for her, or rather for the pleasure of listening to a passage from the Old Testament.

Often, on a Sunday afternoon, we would gather round and conjure the past up in our minds. We knew each other's families and problems in detail, and we would recall the different characters we had met in prison. Of course all our conversation was intermingled with prayer, but we were not able to pray together because of the deafening racket kept up by the ordinary criminals. Each of us therefore would say her prayers at night, when the pain in our limbs, particularly our feet misshapen by the oversized shoes, kept us awake – not to mention the other ills which we knew well and bore in silence. At dawn, after too few hours of sleep, we would wake with swollen hands, incapable of clenching our fists, and fearful that we would not be able to hold a shovel or pick.

God worked real marvels among those of us who trusted in Him. Though we had only the slightest contact with them, we managed to attract, or at least to influence, some of the ordinary prisoners, especially the prostitutes. We heard heart-rending biographies in snatches through the day, on the way to work or during the midday break. We forced ourselves to listen to the accounts of such tragic lives.

'How little love there is in the world! We really have failed to love our neighbours. If I get out of prison one day, I'll devote myself to caring for the suffering.'

'If Richard dies in prison,' said Bintzea, 'I'll give the rest of my life to lepers.'

Thus we still managed to plan – or at least to dream. We

had learned to have confidence in God, to ask Him constantly for strength and spiritual growth and love.

As we worked on the canal I managed to love, genuinely, every one of the women around me, every single suffering person, even though I did not know them. I loved them wholeheartedly. When I first got to Mislea I considered it best to draw close to an individual, to get to know her, to discover what we had in common. Here there was nothing to hold me back. I loved them all, both men and women, because they were human beings. As I loved them I suffered with them. They would confide in me and the sores they showed me hurt me too. I bore other people's pain as though it were my own, though I had scarcely begun to grasp even a small portion of the divine love, to understand the Saviour's sacrifice. In His unique love how much He must have suffered for humanity's woes! Because as a man He had known and loved us, He knew how our sins had to be forgiven so that our suffering and our tears might be blotted out. It is true that sin remains the basis of all suffering. Those who opened their hearts to me had sinned grievously, and their deeds hurt me, but one more sinner would be saved. How much Jesus must have suffered – He who was purity itself for all eternity.

Sometimes I managed to share such thoughts with Bintzea, but more often I talked them over with those who really needed them. I realised that the souls of these women were much more open to goodness and truth in the arid, animal-like existence our work imposed on us than they had been at Mislea. Suffering soaks up such consolation like a sponge. What other consolation can one's soul find than the consolation offered by God?

One afternoon we were assigned to dig holes. I was particularly weary, and waited impatiently for the train which would indicate that work was almost over for the day. I must admit that up to that point I had always been anxious to spot the train. Little Sister Judith came over to offer me a bowl of water. Thanking her, I swallowed it in one gulp and she gave me another. She seemed quite exhausted. Although ill, she would cover miles to take water to the prisoners. Despite her pale face, it was evident she did this gladly, watching happily as each thirsty woman gained some relief through her efforts.

'Work'll soon be over, Sister Judith. Hey, there we are, there's the train on the horizon! We'll be finishing in half an hour, thank goodness!'

'Will you let me say something to you, my dear? I know you'll understand me. I believe that if I accept suffering as I know you accept it yourself – joyfully – then I must not rely on anything in the world outside to give me relief. Why should you wait for the train? Why should you rejoice when another day goes by? I think that for those of us who know exactly how far a joyful acceptance of suffering can take us, it is better to steep ourselves in it, to sink ourselves in it completely, without trying to escape in any way.'

'Yes, except by escaping into the joys of the spirit – the joy of being able to suffer.'

'That's exactly what I meant.'

Sister Judith moved on. She had completely convinced me.

From that day I did my best to turn away from all forms of outside hope. Rumours circulated constantly: for example, that many of us would be released shortly, especially the prisoners such as myself who had received no sentence from the courts. I had not forgotten my resolve never to pray for freedom, but to wait calmly and patiently for God's ruling. Despite everything, my heart trembled at the very mention of freedom. To stay true to the words of Sister Judith I would repeat to myself, 'Seek to plunge yourself in the deepest wells of suffering with joy and utter confidence.' Did I succeed or not? I believe that most of the time, I did succeed, and for me this was a great step forward.

* * *

One Sunday, about three months after I had been posted to the canal, I was given permission to go to the visitors' room.

My darling mother had come all the way from Bucharest to see me and bring me food.

What an event! For the first time in two years, I was going to see my mother again and learn all the news from home.

I tried to dress as well as possible. Someone lent me a scarf which I tied jauntily. Bintzea gave me a white blouse.

We waited an eternity to be called to the visitors' room. At last the great moment arrived! We faced a double grille: our relatives on one side and ourselves on the other, with a militiaman assigned to each prisoner and each visitor. I felt sick at heart as I saw my mother trying to find a place among the people jostling to spot 'their' prisoner and attempting to get a seat opposite. As I drew face to face with her, we found it hard to express ourselves.

'Mummy, forgive me for all that I've done to you,' I stammered.

'Don't ask me to forgive you, my little one,' said mother. She was trying to smile, but tears were running down her cheeks. 'You know how much I love you, how much we all love you. Tell me, how are you? You're thinner. Your face looks pinched.'

'I'm fine, don't worry about me. I work in the open air. Perhaps I've got tanned by the sun and the wind.'

'Tell me the truth: do you get enough to eat?'

'Even too much. You didn't need to make sacrifices to bring me food. We've got all we need, except our freedom of course, but that will come when God wishes it.'

Mother glanced round fearfully, afraid that the soldier would reprimand us for using the word 'God'. But there was such a row going on that even though we were shouting to make ourselves heard, he could not catch what we were saying.

'How about Daddy and my young brother?'

It was her turn to gild the truth.

'They're fine, and they send you all their love . Daddy would have liked to come too, but as we only got permission for one person he let me come.'

'You know, Mummy, all the time I've been here I have

stayed right in God's hands. I've never been so close to Him. I'm praying with other believers, and there's a fantastic atmosphere. Bintzea's here with me.'

Her face brightened.

'The Almighty cares for us so much! I'm so glad that you've found one another. I knew she was here, because Alice and Michael came to see her, but you hadn't yet got to the canal. Praise God that you're together. Do tell her that we're praying for her and for Richard. We pray for all of you. Give her a kiss from me.'

'She kisses you too and told me to ask you to give her love to everyone. How are her family?'

'They're well, but they don't have any news of Richard.'

'Remember, Mummy, the Scriptures say that every pain which now seems hard to bear will one day bring forth fruit. Please think of our current sufferings that way, you there and me here. Nothing is impossible with Jesus. He is present everywhere. He comforts all our pain.'

'I know, darling. But I miss you so much. I can't tell you how I miss you.'

'That's part of the test. But you'll see, we'll be together again, and then we'll be even closer in Him.'

We exchanged a few more words before the end of the interview. I watched as the soldiers savagely shook the 'free' men and women who clung to the bars calling a last few words to their loved ones.

'If they're this brutal with us, what must they be like with you?' cried mother. 'You poor girls!'

'Mummy, don't leave thinking that way. We're not alone here. Jesus is with us, He protects us and gives us strength. You know, except for wanting to be with you, I'm happy here. Don't forget that, please. Read Verse 11 of Hebrews 12 . . .'*

All around me men and women were weeping as we were jostled into ranks to leave the room. In the yard we waved

* 'No discipline seems pleasant at the time, but painful. Later on, however, it produces a harvest of righteousness and peace for those who have been trained by it.' (NIV)

and looked back, just as our relatives were doing, but in fact we could no longer make them out in the tight group which moved away from us, no more than they could tell between us. Then it was over, like a scene from a play. I let myself be led away.

For days I thought of nothing but my family. Back in the dormitory those who had not had a visitor comforted me gently. I sobbed in Bintzea's arms, and she consoled me like a child. Human beings have so much need of love! I pray that I'll never forget that – but it's something that can only be learnt through intense suffering.

I might have said a good deal about life in a forced labour camp. For example, my mother could have learned that I had borrowed a striped jacket from one of the ordinary prisoners. My jacket, like most of ours, was damp. It had rained for days at a stretch. There was no cover on the site. The soldiers had plastic raincoats and tall boots which sheltered them from the rain, but we had to go on working in clothes which soaked up water. Back in the dormitory each evening the political prisoners were not able to get near the metal stove which the other prisoners had taken over. They had the privilege of getting dry wood to burn to dry their clothes, but we were shoved far away from the heat. Even if we were on good terms with some of them, the more hard-hearted would chase us off. As a result we spent days on end with soaking jackets and damp undergarments. If there was wind after the rain (which often happens in the climate of the Dobroudja) our clothes would dry, but we knew too well the cost of this good fortune. The usual result was colds and fevers. But who cared that we caught cold, when there were those suffering from chronic bronchitis and sinusitis, all in pain and soaked to the bone? If at the morning's roll-call you did not have a temperature of at least 38° you were able to work. That is why I took advantage of the fact that I was well liked by some of the ordinary prisoners to borrow a dry jacket for my mother's visit.

As I recall such details among so many others, I realise

that the harsh facts have lost their intensity in my mind. That is why I am trying to retain in these lines only the aspects that have remained unaltered, living, still as fresh within me as when they happened, in particular the wonderful times I spent with Jesus, constantly in His presence, constantly aware of living with Him. The same applies to the unforgettable friendship, the sense of sisterhood which united all those of us who shared the same convictions and the same ideal. Such matters are written indelibly on my soul, and if I write them down it is so that those who still do not know that the happiness of a life given over totally to Jesus can have this same joy.

* * *

Some things were completely unexpected. When we awoke one fine morning we were ordered to stay in our barracks.

'Get your group together. The leader is to collect the bowls, spoons and shoes. She will also make an inventory of the sheets and pillows.'

The woman guard assigned to us set to work with the leader. They attended to the bedding first of all. After we had swallowed our *tertch* the bowls and spoons were gathered up. Then we waited. All kinds of speculations arose, and the women gathered in little groups to discuss the matter. The authorities kept their secret so well I am sure even the soldiers did not know what was up.

By the sun we could tell it was almost midday. All morning we had heard steps outside our dormitory. We realised that other barracks were being emptied and the prisoners taken towards the gate. But what happened then?

I joined the group of nuns. They were the only ones who did not seem in the least worried: they prayed constantly, and I felt calmer near them.

In another corner Bintzea tried to continue with the story of Joseph, but this time I don't think she was able to hold many people's attention. Our seclusion, the bustle outside, the change in schedule, the cataloguing of different items, were all signs of something which affected us directly and would change our destiny at a stroke. That was why I found a greater calm beside Judith. I didn't want to feel worried by thoughts or suppositions or even ordinary human hopes. Judith guessed this and as she continued to pray silently she smiled at me and held my hand.

A large-scale move was under way. We were leaving the canal. Eventually the doors of our barracks opened and we were told to move out. The women waited ranked in eights, and I saw immediately that the political prisoners from other barracks had been mixed with the ordinary prisoners.

On the parade ground officers dashed here and there. One had a list. The women from our dormitory had been gathered in the small area in front of the barracks (there was a similar space before every barracks). The sun shone down on us: it was a fine day, we were on the verge of summer.

'Attention!' shouted the officer. 'When you hear your name, fall in in front of those already in line!'

I glanced in disquiet towards Bintzea and my other friends.

My name was one of the first called. This was only to be expected as the list was arranged alphabetically. But even at the start of the list some were omitted, and I anxiously waited till the last names were reached, as Bintzea would be last of all. She looked at me unhappily, as if she had a premonition of what was coming. The roll was completed without her name being mentioned. I was already in place in the ranks, a good distance away from her and the other members of our group who still stood before our barracks. When the selection was complete, the soldiers gave the orders to move off, and we were roughly separated without a single goodbye, a last kiss. I suffered physically at leaving Bintzea and the others in this fashion.

'Get into line!' screamed a soldier at me, intercepting my wave of farewell to the group of women who still stood petrified on the threshold of the barracks.

We carried painful memories with us away from the

canal, but I could also recall many sublime moments. We had no idea where we were being taken. We only knew that once again we were separated from people we loved, and separations in prison are just as painful as those elsewhere. The links forged under such harsh conditions as we had faced are stronger than death. Man is gifted with an extraordinary resilience: we observed even in atheist prisoners this resistance to suffering, and dignity and courage too. Who knows what efforts they had made to display such qualities? What did it cost them? How much did they suffer? Whereas those who have received the grace of God can come through any test whatsoever, their souls intact, even enriched.

CHAPTER SEVEN

We left the canal just as we had arrived, crammed into the train we remembered all too well. Crushed against one another, deafened by the infernal racket kept up by the prostitutes, we travelled for approximately five days. Because of the crowding and the heat several women spent the journey in a state of almost constant unconsciousness: as for the rest of us, we lost all track of time. Our estimate of five days was little more than a guess.

I found myself not far away from the Catholic nuns, but I had no hope of talking with them. I deeply admired their ability to bear every discomfort without a word of complaint. The prostitutes and thieves quarrelled incessantly, using the coarsest language imaginable, and at each blasphemy or obscenity I glanced in embarrassment towards the nuns. Imperturbable, they paid no attention. The purity of their lives stopped them from understanding the swearing, which simply meant nothing to them. It was just as incomprehensible as insults in an utterly foreign language.

The sudden separation from Bintzea and my other friends had left me very low. A good number had stayed at the canal, but something told me that this time we would not be apart for long: we would soon see one another again. The remaining women would probably be leaving shortly, so perhaps we would find one another in some prison or work camp. I thought of Bintzea, who was very delicate: who would help her now?

In the general noise and discomfort the only refuge was prayer. From time to time I would exchange a few words with those – I won't say near me, but above or below me. The confusion was indescribable. Some of the smallest women had wormed their way up into the luggage rack and managed to stay there by keeping their knees tightly drawn up under their chins. We were all in a stupor. With every motion we felt as though a hundred thousand needles were jabbing us, from the tips of our fingers to the ends of our toes. We all suffered from thirst and headaches. Each day the guard passed in a small parcel of cold food which went from hand to hand until it reached those up in the luggage racks. It was difficult, however, to eat in such postures, with some seated, others on their sides, still others on the knees of those who had found a place to sit. To my astonishment most of the ordinary prisoners, the youngest in particular, found the situation wildly amusing. Water rarely reached the recesses of the compartment: we were given it in bottles, and each prisoner was allowed a single swallow, but some individuals callously drank all they wanted so that nothing remained for the rest. As for the guards, if we asked them for more they refused indignantly, saying they were saving us the trouble of making our way to the lavatory.

I wondered if, when I was freed, I would be able to describe this journey for my family. I came to the conclusion that no description, no matter how detailed and accurate, would be able to approach the terrible reality. It was unreal, impossible to believe, even to those of us who lived through it.

* * *

When we were released from the train at last, we were in a siding in the station at Bucharest North. We must have seemed a comic sight to the guards as we emerged, for they were bursting with laughter. I had to admit that very few of us were walking upright. Most of the prisoners were twisted, bent double, dragging their feet, rubbing their hands and arms.

Nearby, an inspection tour of the railways was under way, and heads appeared at the windows. The officials' attention had been attracted by the noise we were making, which did not stop despite threats from the guards. One of the militiamen trained his rifle on the windows, shouting, 'Get away from those windows, or I'll shoot. What is there to see? These are all women with thousands of deaths on their consciences!'

In reply the windows opened and we were bombarded with bits of paper hastily screwed into balls. They assumed we were all criminals, even the nuns.

Black Marias awaited us nearby. We were piled into them as we had been crushed into the train, pushed and even thrown. Some of us were quite incapable of taking a single step to climb up into the lorries.

With each touch on the brakes we were hurled against the sides or roof of the lorry, and the bodies heaped upon us crushed us all the more. Towards midday we were ordered out into a delightful green field. Over a huge area ranged tall barracks separated by a path. Before them stretched a field full of flowers. The green of the fruit trees and the twittering birds made a peaceful pastoral scene. In the distance we could see the sails of a mill and several solidly built houses with brick-red roofs and little open windows high up in the walls. I could not get used to the idea that we were going to live in the midst of nature, and moreover in real houses. I thought the barracks might serve as sheds and shops and that the roll would be called here before we set off for the houses. The windows were a long way from the ground (as you would expect when intended for prisoners, I said to myself) but they did not have bars. This was an unexpected gift: no more bars, and all the joys of nature. We swapped impressions, concurring that working in the fields, which seemed our likely occupation, would certainly be easier than labouring with stones on the dyke, not to mention those holes we had been digging. The pleasant sun and a light breeze made me long to sit down on the ground and roll around in the green grass.

'Where do you think we are?'

'Not far from Bucharest. We can't have travelled more than three-quarters of an hour.'

'Just think of it: we're not far from home!'

'Sure, for some of you. But how about us? Ardeal and Moldavia are miles and miles away . . .'

'All the same, we're closer to civilisation. No more of that desert round the canal.'

'Where do you think they're going to put the women left behind? From the number of houses here I doubt if there's enough room to hold everyone.'

'There must be plenty of other places where they need field labour. If our working conditions are getting better then there's no reason why it should be any different for the others. There was no rhyme or reason behind the selection.'

'That's true.'

Each flight of fancy was more optimistic than the last. We soaked up the warmth of the sun and filled our lungs with the clean country air. No one took any notice of what was happening around us. It felt so good to relax after that frightful journey and so many months of back-breaking labour on the banks of the Dobroudja.

Our dreams were short-lived. From the direction of the mill appeared a group of civilians and soldiers. As they approached, the guards, who had also stretched out in the sun, scrambled to straighten their garments and stand to attention.

As the group neared us the orders rapped out:

'On your feet! Form a square by columns of ten!'

The guards urged us into a large square, in the centre of which stepped the newcomers. There were quite a few of them but only one held the rank of lieutenant; the rest were junior officers or privates. There were also four civilians, tanned, plump and solid. The officer stepped forward.

'Now listen to me! You're here to work in the fields and gardens. Don't kid yourselves that these are gardens like the ones where ladies scratch the surface with nice little coloured tools. Here you've got real work to do, which will require every ounce of your strength, with set tasks to fulfil. Those who don't work don't eat. The comrade soldiers around us will be in charge of you. None of you will be allowed to speak directly to a civilian. The comrade civilians will show you what to do, but all orders will be transmitted to you through the comrade soldiers. As long as you're here you'll keep strictly to the rules. Every infringement will be severely punished. Got it?'

'Yes, sir!' the ordinary prisoners shouted back together.

The officer noted the silence maintained by the political prisoners. He added, 'The political prisoners to my right, the rest to my left. Move!'

We broke ranks to form two disorderly groups.

'I want those of you who are doctors or nurses to step forwards.'

Dr. Vulpescu moved out, together with two younger prisoners who said they were nurses. They were asked their names, ages and reason for imprisonment. All three had been sentenced by order of the administration.

'Since you're administrative prisoners, that is to say that you haven't been condemned by a jury, your term is elastic: it can be increased or diminished. That will depend on your work and the way you respond to discipline. Doctor, you will stay in the camp, you won't be going to the fields. In any case you're relatively old. The nurses will be going out with the two work groups I'm going to designate.'

The officer then turned to the head guard who had escorted us from the canal.

'How many women do you have here altogether?'

'Two hundred and twelve, Comrade Lieutenant.'

'Put a hundred in one task force and a hundred and twelve in the other.'

'Yes, sir!'

'You've got three barracks to lodge them in, plus one to

serve as a kitchen and one for a hospital. The doctor will also be required to care for the civilian personnel on the farm in the presence of a soldier. Mix the political prisoners and the rest in the dormitories. So that there are no arguments take them in alphabetical order. The doctor will be looking after the prisoners and will come round the dormitories with me each morning on my tour of inspection. Everyone will be required to work apart from those who are seriously ill; in these cases the doctor will take their temperature and confirm that they have a fever of at least 38°. Oh, and one other point. As there are two work groups, there will be two group leaders. Now, allocate them their barracks. There will be no work until tomorrow morning. Fall out!'

The guards who had come with us moved off, apart from the one who had answered the lieutenant's questions. The soldiers who made up the lieutenant's bodyguard took their places.

One of the ordinary prisoners asked a soldier, 'Are you really going to lodge us in these ghastly barracks? Why can't we live in those fine houses?'

'Which houses?'

'The ones over there,' she replied, pointing to the buildings around which we had spun so many dreams.

'Idiot! Those aren't houses, they're pigsties. If you want to live with the pigs you've only got to ask the commandant.'

'Good grief, the pigs live better than people here,' protested the woman.

'Shut your mouth, or you'll feel the back of my hand.'

After this shocking discovery I felt that the most we could expect was a harsh life and backbreaking labour in miserable conditions. As we looked at the rows of barracks we realised that they were just like any others, except that they seemed deserted and long disused.

'Those barracks date from the German occupation,' commented one woman.

'Look at the middle one, the roof's fallen in. We'll get

plenty of fresh air. That's fine now in summer, but what will we do when the rain starts?'

'For the moment let's be thankful that it's fine and warm and that we can lie and bask in the sun for a bit,' said Stella, one of the nurses.

Trying to look on the brighter side we sat down in the grass together, hoping to take maximum advantage of the holiday we'd been granted. We were brought what passed for a meal – cold as ever – but were allowed to drink our fill at a fountain in the middle of the yard. We were overjoyed to have water to wash ourselves, to refresh our tired bodies, to slake our thirst. How full of precious things our daily life is, I thought: we only learn to appreciate them, sadly, when we lose them.

In the meantime the dormitory allocations had been worked out. It looked as though the political prisoners would be more or less together, a prospect which delighted us. Even if we were to sleep in different barracks, we would be neighbours all the same. In the fields, moreover, we would no doubt be working fairly near to each other, and at any rate we would keep in touch. We resolved to observe camp discipline and to set a good example. Then we did our best to persuade the doctor to be as indulgent as possible and to take pity on those who were ill: a number of us suffered from tuberculosis, and one woman with cancer sometimes had severe haemorrhages which prevented her working. We asked the doctor to speak to the commandant about this lady, hoping she might get some kind of job indoors, with the kitchen and maintenance staff. The doctor, however, whom we nicknamed 'Tutza', would not promise a thing.

'Please don't ask the impossible of me. I'll do all I can, but I can't ask favours on my first day here. You know how hard I found it labouring on the canal: I'm getting old and I suffer a good deal. Let me take advantage of the position I've got here.'

'But on the canal,' I replied, 'we made sure you were all right and gave assistance when you needed it. That's why we're asking for your help in return, now that you're able to help us.'

She pretended not to hear and walked off grumbling. We were never without such people among us: we met them everywhere we went.

That afternoon the 'fat cat' civilians returned and ordered us to fall in by alphabetical order as the commandant had required. The first work group was designated, one hundred strong, then the second.

'Forget about your dormitories. When you form ranks, you will take your place in the work group you belong to. Understand?'

'Yes, sir,' we chorused. We were already rested and keen that everything should go well – keen, that is, to avoid any kind of argument.

The commandant asked each group in turn to nominate those they considered suitable leaders. The women in my group put me forward.

'What's your name?'

'Bruteanu.'

'Anything else?'

'Nicole.'

'Nicole? What kind of a name is that? Some kind of fantasy?'

'That's what my parents christened me, Nicolette. The family used to call me Nicole.'

'Stop grinning, the rest of you. Here you'll be called Niculina, get it? That's a good Rumanian name, nothing French about it. That era's dead and gone.'

'I understand, sir.'

He was right. I had never approved of the name my parents had given me. They used to tell me that my godfather had wanted it and that he had chosen the diminutive himself.

'If these women want you as their leader, we'll give it a try.'

This matter settled, we were shepherded off towards the barracks.

One of the ordinary prisoners asked permission to speak.

'Please, sir, there are about fifteen women here with syphilis: they've got running sores on their throats, mouths and bodies. We don't want to be infected by them. When we were on the canal, they were kept isolated from the rest of us. Everyone is in danger while we sleep and live alongside them.'

The commandant thought for a moment, then cursed and made up his mind.

'Step forward, all those with syphilis.'

Approximately fifteen girls moved out with a defiant expression.

'Now let's have fifteen women from Barracks Number One.' (Barracks Number One contained more political prisoners.) 'The fifteen others line up here in front of me.'

Fifteen women from our barracks stepped forward.

The commandant smiled evilly.

'The women with syphilis will take the place of the fifteen from Barracks Number One. That way the political prisoners will be with the syphilitics, and catch syphilis, and the syphilitics will catch politics. Move!'

The fifteen girls came across to join our groups. They would be sleeping and eating with us for a long time.

The commandant found the way he had solved his problem particularly amusing: he burst into shouts of laughter, repeating the rhyming words with great enjoyment. He had clearly just discovered what a poet he was.

When we finally got into the barracks we found platforms along the walls on which lay mattresses, sheets, pillows and blankets. There were even pillow-cases, which pleased us a good deal. Each person had her own mattress. We were not as crowded together as we had been at the canal, where we had never had enough room to stretch ourselves out. The fifteen girls had the tact to stay together at the far end of the dormitory. The few other ordinary prisoners refused to take the places next to them: it was the nuns who took the mattresses adjoining the fifteen, and this Christian gesture made a big impression on the sick women. The rest of us settled in where it suited us, feeling more at ease as we found places for ourselves. The nuns were positioned along the wall opposite me, and I was very glad to have them continually in view, making such a distinct contrast to the fifteen. It was a real blessing for some of those poor girls to be able to talk to the nuns. To show their gratitude the girls would even help the older nuns with their work in the fields when they fell behind. The poor sisters did their very best not to be indebted to anyone, but because they did their work meticulously and conscientiously they were often at the back of the work party, and therefore exposed to the whistles and curses of the guards. At this point the girls would suddenly appear as if by magic and dig the nuns' furrows for them to bring them into line with everybody else.

For the evening meal we were given fresh milk and hot *mamaliga** (a porridge made from barley and chestnut meal). Everything seemed to be working out quite well. We were very pleased. When we left the canal we had been given back our shoes in place of the clumsy boots, and it was wonderful that afternoon to be able to walk around in bare feet, to wash them and let them recover from the swelling which had developed during the rigours of the journey. We had great hopes that all would go well the next day, our first as agricultural labourers.

The commandant ordered the two group leaders to his office that evening. It was in a largish house behind our barracks, where he and his men had their quarters together with a number of offices.

He spoke very reasonably, asking us to do our best to get the maximum work from the women in our charge, and promising that if we produced above the norms he would send in a favourable report so that all our sentences would be reduced. My colleague was completely won over. The authorities had only sentenced her to a year's imprisonment, but she feared that as the sentence was elastic, it

* *Polenta* in Rumanian.

might be extended at the end of the first year. The lieutenant's words were most persuasive. When we returned to the barracks, she repeated his promises to her sister-in-law. Poor women, I thought: they were under so many illusions.

I lasted as leader precisely one week.

I quickly understood that I was no more than a tool in the hands of the soldiers and the civil authorities, and that my role simply consisted of shouting constantly and threatening my companions in suffering. I changed tactics. When I saw women hoeing madly to get ahead and maintain a vast lead over the others, I stopped them, putting the laggards in their places and sending them to the back of the line. In this way we met the norm for several days, but did not pass it. I would have liked to report to the commandant, but was told I would have to wait. The following Saturday I stood once again in the commandant's office.

He lifted his head and looked at me.

'Sir,' I began, 'I've come to tell you that I can no longer carry the responsibility of being a leader.'

'And why?'

'Because I can't agree with the civilians and soldiers in charge of us. I can't ask these women to work their fingers to the bone to keep up with the quantity of work demanded of us. I'm a prisoner like the rest: I've got no right to spur them on. That's why I'm asking you to find another leader and let me work alongside the others.'

'Those women know very well why they chose you. You're indulgent, you're never in a hurry . . . I can assure you there's no lack of candidates. I could find ten, just like that.'

'I don't doubt it. But I'm not prepared to have that sort of sin on my conscience.'

'What's sin got to do with it? Have I made you commit sins? You committed your sins earlier, which is why you're here.'

'I agree, sir, I am guilty of faults, just as we all are, but I don't want to add to the list the sin of physically destroying women who are suffering the same punishment as me.'

'So according to you it's a sin to encourage your companions to work. That means you're breaking the rules. I've already been told that you're advising your fellow prisoners not to work their hearts out.'

'I believe I would be sinning if I continued to order them to do the impossible. That's why I would like to go back to the ranks and work alongside them as best I can.'

'Listen, I've got another suggestion to make. I can see that you have plenty of energy, and they've told me that you're an intellectual. There's a job going in this office. Forget the fields, and come and work here.'

'Thank you very much, sir, but without wanting to offend you, I must refuse your kind offer. I think that it would be more logical for you to choose an older woman to work in the office, someone who is too ill to contribute much as a labourer. I'm still young and strong, and I think that my place is out in the fields.'

He looked at me wryly.

'You're an odd one, aren't you?'

I didn't answer. It wasn't the moment to start a discussion.

'And who would you suggest for the office, for example?'

'Among the political prisoners?'

'Who else do you think I mean? You're surely not going to help the others?'

'I don't make much distinction between them. Everyone here is under the same sentence, and when they're faced with punishment, they're just as equal as when they're faced with death.'

My words pleased Commandant Bulie.

'Choose a political prisoner. They're more educated in any case.'

'Madame Namzache, perhaps. She's fifty-five years old and very delicate, but she's well educated.'

'Right. Get across to the dormitory and fetch her.'

My real life at Ferma Rosia (Red Farm) thus began.

We rose at dawn. We made our beds and were given a large bowl of full cream milk with a hunk of bread. It was not yet daylight. Then came the commandant's tour of inspection, on which he was accompanied by the doctor. We then set off for work in our respective groups: the sister-in-law of the leader of the second group had been appointed in my stead, and both hoped to be freed if we produced well above the norms.

When all was ready we would strike out into the fields. Some hoed, others weeded, others harvested the vegetables. But it was clear that this camp was still being established. Each day some fresh change was made. The soldiers were replaced by female guards, but the outskirts of the camp were still watched by men.

From time to time the lorry would bring in more women, two or three together, from the transit camp at Ghencea. Ghencea was a clearing house which supplied manual labour to a whole series of camps around the capital. This meant we could get news from women who had worked on the canal. A number of these were now at Bragadiru, a vast forced labour camp also given over to agriculture and garden produce. One of the new arrivals had come from there. She had fallen ill, and been sent back to Ghencea, and then by chance had been posted on to Ferma Rosia. We bombarded her with questions, and learnt that many of our comrades were now at Bragadiru, Bintzea among them. She had not been difficult to find. I asked only if there was a small dark-haired woman with a very strong faith and got an immediate response.

'Bintzea? That must be who you mean. Yes, she was there, poor girl, but she was very ill: she kept fainting and there were spots all over her face. They sent her away to the hospital at Vacaresti.'

'When?'

'The last time they came to get labourers. She was at Ghencea and she was waiting for transport to Vacaresti: they took her to Vacaresti the day before I left, together with three other invalids.'

I was saddened to hear that my poor Bintzea was alone and ill. Who could tell where they might send her after some parody of treatment at Vacaresti? I knew very well that no one stayed long at the huge hospital there which took in cases from every prison in the country.

Life was no bed of roses at the farm. Although we worked incessantly from dawn till dusk, our new leader pestered us to hurry, denouncing those who wanted to reduce the pace a little. We scarcely had the half-hour we had been allowed at the canal when the food was brought. As the sun grew hotter, we were permitted to wear our own clothes, which were cooler than the convict jackets – but on the other hand we were not allowed to cover our heads in the fields, not even with a handkerchief.

'What? Do you want to attract the Americans' attention when they fly over to drop bombs on us?'

The poor souls were scared of something which we had long since ceased to hope for.

Each evening we would return to our sheds, dusty and so weary that sometimes we did not even have the strength to wash ourselves or drink the soup which formed our usual meal. We would collapse on our mattresses in inert heaps.

* * *

I could see no way of arranging for Bintzea to be transferred nearer me, yet something told me she would nevertheless turn up. Then, one day, we had a visit.

The doctor who used to serve at Mislea appeared at Ferma Rosia. She had been transferred and was now working at Vacaresti, from where she made trips to camps around the capital. She had come to check on the health of the prisoners at Rosia, removing the weaker ones and replacing them with women still strong enough for manual labour. 'The State doesn't need parasites, but arms able to work!' she would shout. I had heard that this doctor was now at Vacaresti, but had paid no attention.

When she read out the sick list, I suddenly got up and took my place alongside those who wanted to leave the farm on account of various illnesses. These were the women who preferred prison, even the prison at Jilava which was generally considered the harshest, rather than have to face a moment longer the backbreaking labour we endured. When my turn came to speak to the doctor – who had witnessed my unforgettable confrontation with the prison director at Mislea – I realised that she recognised me and was considering me quite pleasantly.

'So what's the matter with you?' she queried, pretending not to know me.

'I've got toothache, and no way to ease the pain. I'd like to have one or more removed, but we don't have a dentist here.'

'Right. You can go and see the dentist at Ghencea. There's no need to take your things with you, only the bare minimum.' (As if the choice bewildered us!) She looked around. 'Get ready, all those who are coming.'

I played along with her and gave my name like the rest.

Two hours later I was at Ghencea. Ghencea was a different kind of hell. Women of all types and social classes, every age and every profession, gathered there to wait for posting elsewhere: the healthy destined for labour camps, the sick for prison.

As I got down from the lorry, the doctor said,

'If there's anything else wrong with you, I can get you sent to Vacaresti.'

'Thank you very much, but my teeth are the only things bothering me. But if you could get a sick prisoner called Wurmbrand transferred from Vacaresti . . . she's my closest friend. I could have her at Ferma Rosia to help her work, and she'd have a chance to see her family.'

I blurted all this out in a sudden access of courage, risking that the doctor would send me packing, since in effect I was asking her to join a conspiracy.

'Still up to your tricks. You'd do better to look after yourself, you're like a ghost.'

'Please, doctor, for Wurmbrand's sake. She's a small brown-haired woman with spots on her face.'

'I know her. I'll try to get her transferred to Ghencea.'

Without another word she turned her back on me and

made her way off towards the camp hospital. That evening none of the doctors called for me.

Going by the experience of former inmates at the camp, I hoped that the lorry which picked up prisoners from all the farms would arrive regularly three times a week to load and unload 'cargo'. Thus no one would arrive the next day. I had at all costs to stay at Ghencea one extra day, though I couldn't spin out a toothache indefinitely. Ferma Rosia was certainly in need of additional labour, and it was therefore possible that a number of prisoners would be headed that way soon. In any case I should not be able to leave until more had arrived from Vacaresti, and that would give me a good chance of finding Bintzea.

The following morning, when an attendant read out the list of those scheduled to visit the hospital that morning, a prisoner in whom I had confided advised me to go out into the yard and thereby miss the roll call.

When my name came up she replied on my behalf, 'She's out in the yard. She couldn't take the pain any longer so she went out into the sun . . . I'll go and fetch her.'

The attendant let it pass without comment: one woman more or less was of no consequence in such a crowd.

That afternoon the attendant came out to find me. I answered his call since I could conceal myself no longer.

'Why didn't you turn up at the hospital this morning?'

My comrade jumped in before I could reply. 'I couldn't find her, sir, she was weeping with pain in a sunny corner of the yard.'

'What am I going to do with you now? You''ll just have to wait for tomorrow morning, the dentist's gone. But don't make me come chasing after you tomorrow.'

'I understand, sir. Thank you very much,' I murmured.

The following day I made my way across to the hospital, stopping before a door labelled *Dental Section.* Inside a woman was screaming like a beast being slaughtered.

As I waited my turn I recalled the frightful toothaches I had suffered at Mislea. I could not stand the pain caused by two teeth in my lower jaw, and as I had no access to any form of medicine a hospital attendant persuaded me to have them out. As he had no kind of dental equipment he took me over to the surgery with three other prisoners. Sitting me down he brought the smallest pair of pliers he could find in his bicycle repair kit, disinfected them and swabbed my mouth with alcohol. Then, with one woman on either arm and the third kneeling before me clasping my feet, he tackled first one molar, then the other. He shifted them a little, then stopped; although they were rotten they were still well rooted. The pain increased as he tugged. I could see from his face that he was really feeling for me. My forehead dripped sweat: my fists tightly clenched, I jerked rigid with each of his attempts.

'Just a little bit more and it will all be over. You'll have no more pain keeping you awake for nights on end. Be brave just a little while longer!'

'Is my hair turning white?' I wondered. Pain seemed to be flooding through my head. I could feel myself trembling right up to the roots of my hair.

'No, your hair isn't turning white, but your face is,' one of my friends told me. 'A few more moments and you'll be all right.'

Those few moments lasted more than two hours, since the attendant operated with a good deal of care. We could both feel the root yielding: he pulled harder, and a molar came free suddenly with a spurt of blood. He took the opportunity to rub my lips and gum with alcohol then gripped the second molar and yanked it roughly out. I didn't know whether I was still sane or going off my head with the pain. I rinsed out my mouth with warm water and sank back inert in my chair. The attendant brought me a bottle of lotion he had prepared in advance.

'Take her back to the dormitory and let her sleep. She should rinse the spot from time to time with this liquid.'

Before I left he slipped me two aspirins he had smuggled into the prison – he too was searched at the entrance to prevent any form of medication reaching the prisoners.

Back in the dormitory I was fussed over and cared for.

My dear sisters in the faith spoilt me with their affection.

Now I was waiting for someone to pull a tooth and not a single one hurt. What could I tell the dentist? In I went. The dentist's room was the size of a large cupboard.

'Which one hurts?' he asked.

I opened my mouth and pointed to a molar at random in my upper jaw. Without further ado he seized a pair of forceps and came over to me.

'Open your mouth,' he said, since I had clamped it shut in fear. 'Open your mouth, so that I can get the molar out.'

'Aren't you going to give me any injection?'

'What injection? Why should I? Are you paying me? Don't you know you're in prison?'

'I know, but I've been working and working gives you certain rights. Surely I can expect an injection?'

'You'll get no injections: the tooth's extracted and that's it.'

'In that case I don't want it out!'

He put one hand on the back of the chair and shoved his knee into my stomach. I clenched my teeth together and shook my head in refusal. He swore at me like a navvy and used a different tactic: his knee still in my stomach, he grasped my jaws so tightly with his left hand that my mouth opened like a little swallow's when its parents feed it. The forceps in his right hand plunged towards my upper jaw. I don't know if it was the molar I had indicated, but all of a sudden he shook one tooth with extraordinary force, bared the root and in three quick movements yanked it out.

Giddy, I heard him telling me to rinse my mouth out over the basin. The top of my head hurt. Dazed, I took a mouthful of water, then made my way out of the dental section and away from his conceit, a handkerchief pressed to my lips. I spat out several mouthfuls of blood before getting to my barracks. I threw myself down on the bed next to my friend and gradually grew calmer. Later I realised that he had not removed all the molar, and with the help of a pair of tweezers and a little mirror secretly lent by a neighbour I took care of the rest myself.

That afternoon it was equally painful. Suddenly, however, the barracks was filled with noise and voices. The guards ushered in about eight women, and from the upper bunk I could spot Bintzea.

'Praise the Lord!' I shouted and hurled myself into her arms.

Our meeting took her so much by surprise that she didn't react at once: in addition she may not have recognised me. There were still signs of boils on her face. She had no idea of where she was, nor why she had been transferred. I obviously knew a good deal more, but it wasn't the moment to discuss it.

The important thing now was to find some way of leaving together with the next batch for the Ferma Rosia: according to our reckoning this would be assembled some time that evening. We had no control over departures, and I was scheduled for an early return to Ferma Rosia – after all, I'd only come to have a tooth out – while Bintzea was listed as bound for Bragadiru.

As a third person played a vital role in helping me leave with Bintzea for Ferma Rosia, and as this person is still alive and not in the free world, I can say nothing further about the happy ending to this episode. However, all went well and somehow Bintzea's destination was changed.

There was general astonishment when I returned from my 'adventure' with my precious trophy.

We stayed constantly together, whether it was picking tomatoes, carrying forty-kilo boxes or doing other tasks. Our circle of 'disciples' widened steadily, and we listened with delight as Bintzea continued with the story of Joseph.

The buildings we had hoped to live in when we first arrived, the sties for quality pigs (destined for export or consumption by members of the Central Committee of the Rumanian Communist Party), had a rather rudimentary drainage system. A ditch approximately one metre deep and two hundred metres long allowed the excrement to make its way down into a large pool on neighbouring land.

After several days of steady rain, during which we

worked on regardless, the mud filled the ditch and blocked the exit so that it was in danger of overflowing.

One morning the cloud cover began to break up. As we were about to set off for work as usual, we saw the farm's chief engineer and the commandant making their way towards us.

'I need fifty women to unblock the ditch from the pigsties,' said the commandant.

'I'd prefer some of the more level-headed ones,' added the engineer. 'I'd like to choose some of the political prisoners for this particular job.'

The order was carried out. The whole of our group was designated, as the lieutenant had often noticed that we were believers and very close-knit.

'Get on with it!'

He lined us up in ranks, added a few more to make up the numbers, and off we went.

The soldiers were waiting for us at the edge of the ditch. Rubber boots were piled nearby, and we did our best to get ourselves shod as well and as quickly as possible among the shouts and threats. It was difficult to find the right size, as the boots had been flung down in disorder. We were given buckets and shovels, and the engineer explained what we would have to do. When we reached the ditch we would have to get down into it, supporting ourselves on the planks which straddled it half way down, and shovel out the filth into the buckets. When they were full other women would empty them directly into the pond, so that 'in a few days the problem should be resolved'.

We were then ordered to move off, but to our surprise none of the guards, male or female, went with us as usual. They took up positions along the ditch a good distance away, to the right of the buildings on the right of the pool.

It wasn't hard to understand why they kept their distance, for as we went forward a foul stench poisoned the air. As the pig dung was several days old it was indescribably offensive. We held handkerchiefs to our noses, but in vain: in any case we should shortly be needing both hands free to work. The group leader, Mrs. Diaconescu, was the only one who could block her nose. Shouting to make herself heard, she indicated who was to step down onto the planks and who was to carry the buckets over to the pond. As we climbed down into the ditch we were caught and enveloped by the horrible stink. Two of my friends fainted, and were carried a little further away. Others, spitting and retching, waited for the job to begin.

Those of us who were able to stand the smell began to shovel out the filth. Since the buckets were on the bank above us we were splattered up to our faces as we emptied our shovels: the excrement fell into our boots and soaked into our clothes. Now the foul liquid and lumps of dung were streaming down our arms. As we disturbed the muck the odours grew stronger: one woman began to vomit, but stuck stubbornly to her task so as not to discourage the others. After a quarter of an hour we were drenched from head to foot with pig filth. Geta, who was gentle and delicate, left the bucket she had been going to empty and rushed away towards the soldiers, and we saw one of the women guards take her by the arm and steer her off to the barracks. That evening we found her suffering from a severe attack of jaundice.

I wanted to wipe my face; it didn't feel especially dirty, but I could see the faces of Bintzea and the rest. But to wipe it would have only made it dirtier, so I gave up the idea.

Human beings can adapt to nearly anything. Most of us worked on steadily, hoping to make an end of the ghastly business. The soldiers had stopped shouting, even when they saw us pausing to catch our breath. Meanwhile a further fifteen women – all political prisoners – had been brought in to help empty the buckets. While one was being carried down to the pool someone else would bring hers to be filled. The earth around the ditch had grown soft, and several times the planks slipped, plunging some of us deeper into the excrement. This made it that much harder to lift the shovels and load the buckets.

At the end of the morning the guards whistled to signal the break and shouted to us to climb out of the ditch and come across to them. But no one was eager to touch the canteen of food.

'I shan't eat pork again as long as I live,' said Stella.

'What are you going to do then with the bacon you received yesterday in your food parcel?'

'The pigs can eat it,' she replied.

We worked on through to the evening, then piled our filthy boots and implements beside the road.

'If there was a good wind it would dry them a bit,' said one guard, rather embarrassed.

No one answered her. Heads down we trudged back towards the barracks.

We had scarcely reached the yard and had not entered the barracks when the women who had jobs 'inside' – in the offices, the hospital, the kitchen – fled as though we were lepers.

'Phew! You smell like corpses flavoured with dung. Don't go into the dormitory in that state. Your clothes are disgusting. Go and have a thorough wash!'

Our friends, who had been working in the fields as usual, brought us our nightgowns so that we could put them on after our wash. We were even given galoshes so that we didn't come in with the shoes we'd worn after the filthy boots.

We ourselves were no longer aware of any smell. Our very skin was soaked with fetid odours. Though we washed ourselves that evening and the two following (they even heated water for us, which normally only happened once a month) we didn't succeed in getting rid of the stench which made lepers of us all.

I shall never forget the three days we spent deep in the pig muck, nor the dignity with which those who could tolerate it accepted the task. I will never forget, either, the way our dear nuns – the only ones who would come near us when we returned to barracks, words of encouragement on their lips – assured us they were praying for us. They even brought us, from heaven knows where, fragments of scented soap.

* * *

We grew accustomed to life at Ferma Rosia: a pattern of days of backbreaking labour interspersed with others which offered some respite. As the summer drew on the work grew harder; the suffocating heat and the exaggerated norms exhausted us physically. Our group leader railed at us to meet more and more unreasonable targets: in one month's time her year of 'administrative' detention would be over, and the commandant had promised that she would be freed on the appointed day, together with her sister-in-law.

One Sunday morning, a week before their sentence was up, the commandant made us form a square so that he could read out the names of those to be released from the list submitted by the Ministry of the Interior. Six ordinary prisoners were due to be set free, but he made no mention of the sisters-in-law. Our group leader went over to the office to find out what would happen to herself and her relative, and to general astonishment was told that in both cases the sentence had been extended by one year, as the authorities had decided that they were not yet entirely re-educated.

'But you promised us that if we kept the rules and produced top quality work, we would be released, perhaps even before the end of our sentences,' said Mrs. Diaconescu with the courage of despair. 'You were going to send a favourable report to the Ministry . . .'

'Silence! I'm not accountable to you, and the Minister doesn't give reasons for his decisions. That's all. You'll do a further year: it's not the end of the world.'

The same evening we found Mrs. Diaconescu at the end of the yard, hanging from a tree. Luckily she was brought round. After that, although they had been taught the worth of the authorities' promises, the two continued to heap work upon us. No matter what arguments we used, they were not to be dissuaded from exploiting their fellow sufferers without mercy.

I looked upon them with pity, thinking how deeply rooted is human stubbornness. It hurt to see how obsessed and uncaring they were. Together with the doctor they made up the roll of individuals without the slightest altruism that I met during my years in prison. I even got the impression that those in charge of the camp scorned them secretly. Though I have had no contact with them since my release, I still dare to hope that in easier circumstances they have repented of their wrong.

One day we heard that major changes had taken place in the government and that the Minister of the Interior had been replaced. All kinds of political news could arouse our imaginations, but none could get us enthusiastic. We knew all too well that the machinery of the State was so well organised and made up of so many elements that one departure or disappearance could do nothing to improve our situation.

However, the change of minister had certain long-term effects on the prison system which became apparent very slowly. For one thing the investigation into my case was re-opened. One day the notorious black limousine drew up on the road bordering the field where we were working. At that distance I could just pick out two civilians, who after conferring together made their way towards my group. The guard called me over and told me to collect all my possessions.

I was leaving. Where was I going? How long would I be separated from these women I loved like sisters?

Under such circumstances you are given neither time nor permission to say the briefest goodbye: you are not even allowed to glance around. It is as if a thick curtain falls to separate what has gone before from what is to come. I followed the guard, knowing that loving glances were accompanying me, even if my companions were pretending to look elsewhere; I knew too that they were praying for me. Everyone knew that there was no likelihood of my being released: a further investigation, after so long a break, meant that in effect I was being rearrested.

I travelled with the two civilians back to Bucharest. We didn't exchange a word. The countryside, at the height of the summer, was quite superb, especially when viewed from a comfortable seat in the Ministry's Mercedes. I tried to store as many scenes in my mind as possible, so that I would have some kind of supply when locked in my cell. As we arrived in the suburbs I was handed the inevitable felt goggles and I donned them with a dexterity born of long experience.

'Were you arrested some time ago?' asked one of the men.

'Yes,' I replied dryly.

We soon arrived. The town was buzzing with life and movement: we were right in the centre. This time the enquiry would obviously be held at the Ministry of the Interior.

We went straight down to the first basement, where my photograph was taken, together with my fingerprints (for the first time). An officer guided me down a very long corridor like a mausoleum: not a whisper, not a word. The guard and I seemed to float along on our felt slippers. I found the slippers a blessing, compared with the heavy shoes I wore for working the soil or for building the dykes which watered the fields. They recalled the comfort of home in the evening after a day's shopping . . .

At the end of the corridor the guard pressed my arm to turn me.

We seemed to cross a room and enter a further corridor. Immediately afterwards we halted, and a few seconds later I heard a lock turn. The felt was removed from my eyes.

In the cell stood three women, each as wraith-like as the next. They seemed drained of all strength, as if they had been subjected to harsh interrogation and severe punishment. Before he withdrew the guard turned to me.

'You can stay on your bunk until you're called to the office.'

The door shut and the bolt was slammed hard home.

Suddenly I found myself in the arms of one of the three tortured women. It was Galia. I had been separated from her when I left Mislea, and had heard nothing further about her, neither at the canal nor at Ferma Rosia. Her face was aged and dry, but now it lit up with joy. As we embraced each other I realised that she was leaning on me with all her weight. We quickly drew apart; at the Ministry, as in every prison, the spy-hole was checked regularly. However, the experiences she and the others had undergone gave us material for a prolonged whispered exchange of news: we described everything that had happened since our separation.

Galia introduced the other two: peasant women who had been accused of helping the partisans, and whose husbands and sons were now hiding out in the mountains. I would have liked to go on standing near Galia so that I could feel closer to her and allow her to tell me about the trials she had undergone and was still enduring, but I had to stay on the edge of the bed so as not to arouse the guard's suspicions. In turn she asked me about other companions at Mislea, of whom she had heard no news: we switched rapidly from subject to subject. Though the poor woman was utterly exhausted, she summoned up the strength to speak. The surprise and joy of our meeting had put a little colour back into her cheeks.

'The only things which have kept me going are prayer and reciting passages from the Bible. The other poor wretches who have passed through this cell have gained strength from this too. And the two friend with me now have been absolutely marvellous.'

'Oh,' said one modestly, 'we're just simple peasants. We've got no education. While we're suffering here we go on hoping that the Almighty will take pity on us and our families, but above all on our dear country. A curse has fallen on her. Galia has given us lots of encouragement and comfort. We pray God will help her find her children and all her family again.'

'For some time now they have been getting much harsher,' continued Galia. 'We don't know what's happening, but we get the impression that they're hustling up the enquiries and are anxious to close the dossiers. They've never been so hard on us as they have these past few weeks.'

'I think it's probably because there's a new Minister of the Interior,' I said. 'I heard it at work. The new man probably has different plans.'

'Yes, that must be it,' said Galia. 'I understand now.'

The others nodded.

'I'd have been lost without the Word of God', said one.

Galia stood close to my bed, and from time to time we found ourselves gripping each other's hands. 'I hope you don't stay here long,' she told me. 'It'll be better for you at the farm. Of course, I'll find it hard to lose you again.'

'But I've scarcely arrived! What makes you think that I'll be leaving?'

'You've come from a work camp, and they'll send you back to work after a further enquiry. That's what's happened with all the women they've brought in from the labour camps. They never stay more than a week.'

'Who can tell what they're planning? Perhaps someone has confessed something, or perhaps they want to involve me in some sort of trial . . .'

* * *

My interrogation began that night. For two days they refrained from punishing me. During the first night they made a general reassessment of my dossier.

After a week they asked me to acknowledge certain 'facts' in the dossier. They pretended that 'someone', recently arrested, had made a statement on this subject and had said that I, among others, had been party to the information. It didn't even occur to me to confirm or admit what was no more than a straightforward lie. As a result I was kept on my feet all day.

In this I found a kind of satisfaction: I had been embarrassed at being allowed to sit while my companions had to suffer so much. In fact Galia in the meantime had been permitted to lie down, as she had started to faint. However, the peasants were kept on their feet for three or four days at a stretch without more than twenty-four hours' break.

When we were allowed to sit or lie down, our food ration was automatically reduced. Our share of blows, however, was never cut. There were 'specialists' in this field, who would be summoned at night to beat us with rubber truncheons. In addition some of the investigators would strike us themselves, aiming for our mouths, heads, and kidneys.

Then the two peasants were taken away: we were never to learn what became of them. Sometimes life will separate for ever people who have formed lifelong bonds. But memory is a faithful witness, and preserves intact the happy times spent with those we love, such as those two strong, wise peasant women.

To fill the two spare places in our cell, the authorities brought in two new women, both middle-aged. They did not know each other and introduced themselves as soon as the guard closed the door: Otilia and Sanda. As they had only been imprisoned for a few days, the more talkative told us all the latest political news. The other, who suffered a good deal from a liver complaint, stretched out on her bunk.

Several hours later, when the chatty lady had run down, she looked across at Galia. 'Aren't you tired? You've been standing since we came in.'

'We're very tired indeed, but the interrogators have ordered us to remain standing.'

'Oh!' said Otilia, with a worried expression. 'But why do you let them do this to you? If I were you I'd lie down.'

'It's not that easy. If we lie down, the guard who snoops on us every minute will come in and make us get up.'

'And if I don't obey?'

'He'll tickle you with his truncheon.'

'But he won't kill me?'

'He wouldn't go that far, but he'd get you off your bed by dousing you with a bucket of cold water.'

'Or boiling water,' I added.

'In that case we'd better make the most of things while we aren't required to play statues: I'm going to bed. Sanda was quite right to lie down at once . . . Oh! It's filthy! Good Lord . . . I shall certainly resist those brutes with all my strength. In any case I've done nothing. They won't break me easily, that's for certain.'

Galia and I exchanged glances. These women didn't know what it meant to tempt fate.

That evening the two new arrivals were taken before the interrogators in charge of their cases. They left the cell one after the other, led by a guard, the inevitable black blindfold over their eyes.

They returned at dawn a few minutes apart. The authorities closed their torture chamber very punctually. It was a terrible moment: in their wretched expressions, the marks left by the clubs, their dishevelled hair, the blood which ran down their legs and faces, we could see a mirror-image of ourselves, and it horrified us.

That was only the first night.

Otila had been ordered to spend the whole day standing. She began to shriek and batter the door with fists and feet. and Sanda followed her example. The racket set up by the overwrought women spread to the occupants of other cells, and frightful cries arose from all quarters. Men and women who normally only groaned and sobbed began beating on the doors and walls with their bowls, screaming insults at the police and the government. Galia and I were the only ones who did not take part in the furious demonstration.

Within a few minutes the commandant arrived with all his men. Clubs and fists rained down throughout the cells, and the two instigators received their full share. They grew calmer and retreated to the far end of the cell. Every door was locked once more.

'Scum! Liars! Enemies of the people! You'll get just what

you deserve!' shouted the commandant at the top of his voice.

The two women were left in peace for the rest of the day. They lay down on their bunks and even managed to sleep. Later that night Galia came over to me, and we thanked God for the respite He had given us after the rebellion.

The next day was wonderful, for not a soul disturbed us except at mealtimes, when we were insulted and treated roughly. Otilia and Sanda ate their daily ration eagerly.

'You see the results of standing firm?' said Otilia proudly. 'Thanks to me, we can all enjoy a little peace!'

'A life of luxury,' muttered Sanda. 'I think it's the calm before the storm. They'll have other treats in store for us.'

'If they beat me I'll come back at them as I did yesterday. I know perfectly well I'm innocent.'

'We all are,' replied Sanda. 'Let us be thankful for this respite, whether we're innocent or not. As for them, they need victims, and they imprison the ones who seem dangerous to them. That allows them to strengthen their regime. They want confessions, whether they're sincere or not.'

As the second evening drew quietly in, a foreboding of evil hovered over us. Otilia grew strangely agitated.

'We won't get through tonight without some sort of disaster, especially in my case,' she muttered. 'I'm afraid.'

A few minutes later the guard opened the door. He crossed straight to Otilia, fastened the goggles and took her by the arm.

'Move!'

Each of us in turn left the cell to spend the night under hellish, pointless interrogation.

At dawn we were astonished to see Otilia, the last to return to the cell, in the grasp of two guards. She was limp and could hardly stand, her head sagging on her chest. She seemed to have been drinking. As the guards laid her on the bed they told us:

'She's to stay asleep. The rest of you, back to your routine – bosses' orders. Get to it!'

Although our feet were by now so swollen they were

bursting from our shoes and made walking difficult, we were concerned about Otilia, who was in a deep sleep and muttered constantly.

We walked one behind the other, which allowed us to talk quietly together.

'I know what they've done to her, the wretches,' said Sanda. She explained that they would have used injections based on phenothiazine or similar products which among other things wipe out the will and leave the victim like a toy in their filthy paws – a nothing, an empty envelope lacking opinions and personality.

'That's not possible!' exclaimed Galia.

'Yes, I'm afraid it is. I've known about these drugs for a long time. I've talked about them with friends who are doctors or chemists. The chemical formula for the various "zines" was discovered some years ago, and it's been improved since then. For instance, Cardinal Mindszenty was treated this way. This kind of drug induces such severe depression that you are left without the slightest will to resist . . . it makes you reveal your most private secrets.'

'It's ghastly!' said Galia. 'Perhaps she hasn't admitted everything yet. We'll know when she wakes up. If they call for her again, it'll be because they aren't satisfied with her first reaction. Otherwise . . .'

About four o'clock two guards came with a stretcher to take her away. We heard nothing further about her.

The only explanation which stood up was the one Sanda offered. From that day onwards Sanda shut herself off, silently following the routine without a word of complaint, but towards evening she would become nervous and irritable, talking of Otilia and saying that she feared the same fate.

The tragic day arrived. Sanda returned from the interrogators with swollen eyes, trembling like a cornered animal.

'They've arrested my son. Yes, he was there in the next room, they left the door open. He was begging me, "Tell them everything, Mother, be sincere, they'll only let us go if you admit everything!" I couldn't hold back any longer, and I started screaming, "Let me see him! My darling boy! Let me see him and I'll admit anything you want." They told me it was impossible, but they asked him to repeat what he'd said. "Tell them everything, Mother . . ." he started again, and I think I fainted. So it was all over, they'd got him. My lovely son! My lovely son!'

As the cell grew lighter we could see that Sanda had a yellow tinge to her skin and the whites of her eyes.

Galia rapped on the door, and the guard came in to inspect Sanda. Half an hour later a nurse was brought.

'This patient is suffering a sharp liver attack,' she said.

She filled a syringe to give her a soothing injection. Sanda's voice rose in a terrified cry.'

'No! Don't inject me, no injections, you pigs! I want to keep my senses, I don't want to be driven mad because of you. Get out of here, you criminals!'

The nurse explained to her that the injection was a sedative to help her through the attack.

'Liars, crooks! I don't want any injection! You've taken my son away, don't take my reason too!'

The guard came across to the bed, held the sick woman still, and she was given the injection despite her cries. The poor creature struggled briefly, then fell asleep.

At ten o'clock that night she suddenly leapt from her bed and made her way over to the door as though she was sleep-walking. She knocked, and the guard opened it.

'Take me to the interrogators,' she said. 'It's urgent. I want to tell everything.'

She had been swayed by the stories she had heard of the tortures that took place in Communist prisons. Otilia's case had badly shaken her, as had her son's arrest, and she was desperately afraid of the infamous injection and its disastrous results. Suffering from fever, and the weakness brought on by the injection she had received during her liver attack, she had become convinced that the syringe had contained the same chemicals as those which had been given to Otilia and to so many others. She was in very low spirits, especially after hearing her son's voice, and she believed that all will to resist had been taken from her. She felt that she had really been drained of physical strength and forced to admit everything to her torturers.

The full weight of her tragedy did not fall on her, however, until she had admitted all the evidence against herself, her son and the others about whom she had been questioned. When she had signed the statements, the inquisitors told her in great amusement:

'Come on, you can see your son now.'

Overcome with happiness she rushed into the next room, but there was no one there. As she looked across to the door through which she expected her son to enter, she heard his voice begging her, 'Tell them everything, Mother . . .' It was coming from a tape recorder.

The interrogator 'confessed', shaking with laughter.

'The police make a practice of telephoning suspicious characters. Men and women are thus drawn into harmless conversations. During this their voices are recorded: then specialists who can imitate them read texts prepared by the police into a tape recorder with the exact inflexions of the person under surveillance. That was the trick we played on you, by making you think that it was your son who was speaking. After that, you confessed, on your own initiative, under the effect of no more than a sedative. Now we'll be able to arrest your son. He will also confess everything, and he'll be sentenced at the same time as you. That may be the last time you'll see him. Your son is a miserable criminal who has plotted against the Socialist State and against the workers. And you knew everything he was doing!'

Sanda scarcely had the strength to tell me what had happened. After that she fell silent once again, and no one was able to rouse her. She would move her lips, and talk with invisible people. Shortly afterwards she suffered a real mental collapse and was shut away in a psychiatric ward in the Ministry of the Interior.

A few days later I also left the cell.

* * *

When I reached the farm everyone was out working. I paid a visit to the infirmary hoping to find someone to talk to and who might give me some news, but apart from the doctor there were only a few invalids, one of whom I didn't know. The doctor introduced her to me: her name was Eva Hecht. She had just arrived at our camp after a year in solitary confinement at Malmaison Prison. She did not have a great deal to say and was also suffering from a high temperature after a bad attack of sunstroke. For some reason, I felt strongly drawn to her.

My friends and I were reunited when they returned from work. It all seemed a delightful dream. I talked with them, Bintzea particularly, far into the night, already feeling half at home. Our love for one another filled us with life and high spirits. Only one shadow fell in our meeting: the thought of Galia and those like her who suffered in the basements of the Ministry of the Interior. We prayed for those, wherever they were, who were undergoing interrogation. We knew that torture and solitude heaped one upon another could quickly drive a person mad. The women were stunned to learn Sanda's story: the only thing we could do was continue in prayer.

I was still being questioned. Sometimes, when the matter under discussion was of secondary importance, two policemen would come out to the farm and interrogate me in the commandant's office. These periods of questioning were far easier to bear, as I felt safer at my workplace where I could be certain of seeing my companions each evening.

It was usual in the different prisons to say nothing whatsoever about your interrogation, not even to your closest friends. I always felt this was the wisest course; say nothing and hear nothing about each person's case. Sometimes a prisoner would feel the need to talk about something particularly on her mind, and then I would let her speak, but advise her never to repeat what she had told me. There were spies everywhere, and it was perfectly easy to create dire trouble for someone without wishing them the least harm.

I shall never be able to forget two friends who were in one prison I passed through. They were quite inseparable. One had been sentenced to ten years, and the other to three. The latter, who had been a journalist, admitted to the other shortly before her release that she had been given a relatively light sentence because she had held up under questioning and had managed not to implicate two other people. These had remained at liberty, and she had only received three years. Her 'friend' listened to every detail and remembered everything, including the names. Marinella, the journalist, left prison on the appointed day, but not for freedom: she was bound for the Ministry of the Interior. There, faced with the whole situation – every secret she had entrusted to her 'closest friend' – she was forced to admit everything. The people she had mentioned were arrested, and at the trial each received a ten-year sentence. That was the result of trusting someone blindly.

As far as I was concerned, Marinella's plight served as a grim but valuable lesson. After what happened to her I always considered that any discussion must avoid precise details: you cannot be too careful in a totalitarian police state. A lawyer once confided to me that one day, he believed, it would become dangerous even to think. 'Today science can bring to light your most intimate thoughts and feelings.'

Fortunately cases of this kind occurred fairly rarely in prison. Such betrayals should not blind us to the exemplary character of the majority, and some examples of self-denial ought to go down in history.

My dear friend Christine, whom I shall never forget, is a case in point. She came from a provincial town, where she had belonged to a right-wing group. At Mislea she was converted, and came to see the vanity and worthlessness of the efforts she and her companions had made to serve what they described as 'the cause'. Christine became very active among her former political comrades, and several ultimately admitted that exaggerated stances and a false mysticism can destroy rather than build up. Together they regretted many of the errors they had made, and one day Christine said to me:

'How can I believe that God has forgotten what I did? Look, I forgive those who sin against me, I don't bear grudges against them, but facts are still facts. The further I go in the Christian life, the more my murky past fills me with remorse.'

Only twenty-six, Christine already had a stormy history. Her mother had suffered badly from a nervous illness, and her father had taken her mother's place; but, sadly, he died while still quite young. After his death Christine and her brother were brought up by strangers. They proved brilliant students, but once at university allowed themselves to be drawn into politics. Some time later they were arrested. They left behind them their sick mother and their grandmother, helpless in the face of such traumas.

'I so much wish I could make some kind of sacrifice for the Lord,' she told me. 'I want to prove how loyal and faithful I am to Him . . .'

'He can hear you. He knows that your words come right from your heart. You can be sure He'll test your faithfulness, don't you worry.'

'I want to suffer for Him, to be here because I've preached His Word, not for some political reason . . . I want to suffer for Him alone.'

While she was telling me one afternoon about some of the matters which weighed on her mind, a warder came to take her to the prison's office block. I waited anxiously. However, towards ten that night she returned to the dormitory, radiant, her eyes gleaming, her step confident. She had changed completely.

As soon as we were alone she whispered everything that had happened. Two officers from the secret police were waiting in the office. They told her, very courteously, that they had come some distance, from her home town, to bring her a letter from her mother. The letter was indeed signed by her mother and ended with several shaky lines from her grandmother. The two women begged her to be sincere, co-operative and pleasant with these two gentlemen who had visited them before going to the camp at Targsor, our current abode.

'You've been in prison for six years now, miss, and you're serving a heavy sentence. Your mother and your grandmother have suffered terribly. Your brother is still in prison. Your mother, who is waiting for you at home, has begged us to come to see you and to persuade you to be helpful. Unfortunately we have to obey our superiors . . . so we have to specify the conditions under which you will be freed.'

'What conditions?'

'It's like this: in order to get you out of prison and to guarantee you a position as a teacher, to return you to normal life, we just want you to be completely open with the police and to tell us all about those who are still opposed to our party and who are plotting riots and acts of sabotage in collaboration with the West . . . We also want you to tell us about the youngsters who belong to these organisations, and the ones who cling to superstitions about God, and other similar nonsense.'

'Did my mother really ask you to suggest this to me?'

'As you can imagine, she's frankly desperate to see you again.'

'Gentlemen, I utterly refuse your rotten suggestions!'

'You're not only being tough with us, you're being particularly hard on your mother. Do you want to make her go on suffering?'

'Believe me, I feel very sorry for her in her misery . . . but when you present me with such conditions, gentlemen, I prefer to know that my mother is languishing far away from me than to make so many other mothers suffer and weep because of my cowardice. My conscience won't allow me to take part in this kind of grim game. I'm a Christian!'

* * *

Autumn slowly gave place to winter. The cold grew more penetrating, the rain heavier. We would return from work utterly soaked, our clothes wet, to find that our beds were damp because of the rain which dripped through our barracks' broken roof. We tried all kinds of devices to stop the holes, but if the rain was really hard we were wasting our time.

The barracks stank because of our permanently soaking clothes and the damp which penetrated the beds and coverings. The improvised toilets overflowed. The girls in the barracks who suffered from syphilis continued to go about in bare feet and brought in the filth from the latrines mingled with mud from the yard. There was less and less food. Earlier we had been able to enjoy tomatoes and other vegetables which had given us some strength, but the harvest was finished now. The sun had disappeared, leaving a depressing pervasive greyness.

When one of us received a visit, however, it encouraged us all. One day Michael, Bintzea's son, came to see his mother. At the Ferma Rosia such visits took place in a shed in the pig yard. Those of us who tried to follow what happened in the visiting room from our barracks could not see very much – except perhaps the silhouette of the visitors – but we still felt as though we were taking part. When the long-awaited interview ended, after about ten minutes, everyone would have a store of kind words and condolences for those who had just been so brusquely cut off from their family without even embracing them or learning in detail what was becoming of them. Those who received visits on Sundays always returned to the barracks in tears.

Michael was a tall thin youth, who had undergone a great deal for an adolescent his age. Keen on culture and music, and eager to succeed in life, he had known misery from his earliest years, and in particular had suffered by not being allowed to go to school with other youngsters his age: he had been banned on account of his parents (his father had been arrested when he was nine, then his mother). When he visited the Ferma Rosia Bintzea learnt that he had to work for his exams by taking special lessons. Although Alice, the loyal friend who had cared for Michael for years and was like a second mother to him, had assured Bintzea that her son was handling a job and his studies without difficulty, she was not convinced.

'Can you imagine,' she asked me sadly after Alice and Michael had visited her, watching them walk away, 'can you imagine how hard it must be for them? Michael is so thin that you can see right through him . . .'

'He's certainly working hard. But I'm sure that Alice is doing all she can to feed him. He doesn't lack anything essential.'

'I know. Alice is quite capable of going without herself to look after him. But I'm worried about my boy. You can see he's suffering.'

'That's only to be expected. He's also suffering because you are. He's old enough to understand what happened to you, to you and others like you.'

But Bintzea's momentary darkness had lifted, giving place to a broad smile. The hope that always lived in her re-established itself above the concerns that had troubled her briefly.

'Why should I get so upset?' she mused. 'We have a Lord in Heaven and we're all in His hands. In Him Michael has a father and mother who are far finer than Richard and I.'

She found consolation in this reflection.

My turn came on another occasion. For the first time my dear father came to visit me, together with my mother, whom I had already seen when I was working on the canal. They were laden down with food, which they must have had to carry a considerable distance. I saw at once that my father, who at the time of my arrest had seemed in fine fettle and excellent health, had aged and grown weaker: he even needed a cane.

I felt such remorse for my parents' state. They had endured all kinds of suffering because of me over the last few years. Poor people, I thought, what sorrow I've given you!

'Daddy, you're so tired,' I got out in a voice choked with tears. 'You look so weak and you must have found it terribly difficult to get here. Please forgive me. It's all my fault.'

'Just forget about my stick and this weakness of mine. It comes to all of us, and I'm not as young as I was. I feel fine.'

As he spoke he flexed his arms to show how fit he was, then laughed, and his calm eyes lit up, casting a light into my heart. Mother looked at me sorrowfully.

'It's better for you here in the open air, isn't it, dear?'

'Certainly. You know, I've been out in the open all summer, in the sun: I've been able to get plenty of vitamins . . . but how about yourselves? Please tell me the truth.'

Father broke in before my mother could reply.

'We're fine. We're living with Mircea (my uncle, who had offered them a roof after they had been thrown out of their lodgings). We all eat together. Everything's going well, except that we miss you. We're all waiting impatiently for you to come home to us.'

I didn't press them with further questions. When visitors came everybody played a part: everything was fine, it was all going well – the whole object being to give one another mutual support. We did not mention the real problems, or no more than hinted at them. The time we were allowed for the interview slipped away like a dream. We did our best to encourage one another, expressing hopes that we would soon meet again and restating our conviction that each of us should place his trust in God.

They left. My father did his best to look cheerful, but it was clear that he would have to pay for the effort once he had passed the prison gate – after which they would have two kilometres to walk to the nearest bus.

I confess that deep sorrow overwhelmed me as I bade them farewell. If it had not been for my faith I might well have done something desperate. I felt so guilty: they were in this predicament because I had refused to listen to my mother's advice (which I have already mentioned, and which came constantly to mind). I was bitterly sorry for the many times I'd left the house to enjoy myself with others my own age, and my father had asked, 'Aren't you eating with us this evening? Surely you're not going to leave me, you're the light of my life!' How often had I refused him the pleasure of seeing me? Now I would have given practically anything not be separated from him again. If only I had been able to make him happy in his old age.

* * *

Christmas drew near, and the magic of the festival began to stir even in our grim camp. Despite our frozen limbs and faces stung by the keen winds, our hands stiff with cold on the picks and shovels, our feet swollen with chilblains, we felt that Christmas was not far off, floating mysteriously above the heavy clouds. Though we were cut off from the multicoloured twinkling of the shop windows and streets, though our horizons were the muddy or frozen wastes, though we were far from the peaceful warmth and the scent of delicacies being prepared in each Christian household; though we were surrounded each night as we returned to our dark barracks by the ugly smell of our clothes, perpetually damp, and the stench of our unwashed bodies – despite it all we still felt that Christmas was near. Our thoughts and dreams took flight: we joined the Magi or the heavenly hosts, hurrying with them to reach the crib, to kneel and offer gifts to the baby Jesus, the gold, frankincense and myrrh distilled from our pain and tears . . .

Long before the first snow fell we had all been out looking for dry branches, shavings, pebbles and pieces of straw. This treasure, so carefully gathered, would be secretly transformed through the ingenuity of a few skilful individuals into a crib for Christmas Eve. Its famous characters would be moulded from a mixture of bread crumbs and earth, tinted with carefully conserved toothpaste and the black or dark red polish squirrelled away by those of us who had the 'honour' of polishing the guards' boots . . . We even had a Christmas tree. We tied together branches, trimming them to the shape of a pine and draping around them a few wisps of green wool from a scarf which Helen had unravelled for the purpose. As for the Christmas cake, this would be prepared from slices of maize loaf, our 'daily bread', sprinkled perhaps with a light coating of sugar.

Maybe these feverish preparations will seem laughably primitive to those who have known neither prison nor labour camps. We were well aware how naïve our joy and our actions must seem: but such a childlike spirit allowed us nevertheless to perceive the mystery and tremendous joy of Christ's birth that much more clearly. How wonderful it was to wait for Holy Night! We were overwhelmed by our sense of togetherness, of our unity in the Christian faith. It was immensely comforting to know that despite the severe restrictions imposed by the camp authorities, our faith and love for Jesus bound us together and gave us the courage to resist them. A shiver passed through us as we waited to sing softly round the crib: 'Unto you is born this day in the city of David a Saviour, which is Christ the Lord . . .'

* * *

It happened while we were at lunch that day, the sixth before the festival itself. We were struggling against the wind which flung practically all the soup from our bowls straight into our faces, and thus failed to notice the all-too-familiar black limousine. It drew up on the road which, perhaps two hundred metres away, bordered the patch of ground where we had been working. When the camp commandant came up to us, accompanied by two men we did not know, our hearts practically stopped. The commandant snapped my name, adding:

'Fetch everything you've got and follow me.'

I looked around at my friends, seeing the anguish and worry in their eyes. Such an abrupt departure in that black limousine could mean nothing but a fresh investigation. The comrades nearest me had only the chance to whisper 'God go with you', 'Keep your courage up'. Unfortunately I was not able to reply: it was too risky to talk at such moments, especially for the ones who remained behind. As far as I was concerned, I knew perfectly well what was in store.

'Get moving!' shouted the commandant.

As I stuffed my bowl and spoon into my bag I managed to look each woman in the face one final time. Human eyes can say so much: they can articulate the whole world's suffering, but also love, hope and trembling good wishes for a blessed Christmas.

After several hours' journey I found myself in a strange room, a basement. The walls were particularly horrible: circular holes, the same width and depth as a litre bottle, pocked each surface in a symmetrical pattern. A military-style bed, table and chair seemed lost in the large room. There was no window. The blinding light bulb and the strange round holes were terribly tiring on my eyes, which had grown used to the goggles' darkness during my journey.

My thoughts whirled, and I began to be really afraid. I had no idea where I might be. The silence of the grave seemed to permeate the whole building. I had no means of telling the time, and therefore could not know whether I might lie down: whether, indeed, the whole affair was real, or a nightmare. Finally physical exhaustion took over and I dozed off, sitting on the bed. I did not regain my senses until the door opened and the guard came in, holding out the inevitable goggles. Jumping to my feet, I let him cover my eyes. He grasped my left elbow to guide me. As we followed the corridors, climbing and descending staircases, I recovered my self-control, regaining the frame of mind I had maintained during previous long nights of questioning. As on earlier occasions, the words of the psalm came to me, and I repeated them all the way to the door of the office where the investigation would take place. 'The Lord is on my side, I will not fear; what can man do unto me? The Lord is on my side, He is my helper, and I shall gloat over my enemies.'

* * *

I would prefer to keep silent about the enquiries which began that night, and continued for a further twenty days. I will only say that this period was the hardest I experienced through all my years in prison. What, in any case, could I add to the details so many others have offered concerning the interrogators' barbaric 'modern' methods?

At my first meeting with the secret police I learned that I was in a special villa far away from any other dwelling. 'This will allow the enquiry to proceed more rapidly,' they assured me.

Every method practised today, therefore, could be used to make the prisoner confess. There were no restrictions in this secluded place, where the interrogators were accompanied only by two trusted guards and a few senior investigators. No one would know whether I came out alive, or died in this house of misery. No one would hear my cries, no nearby prisoner would tremble, or pray to God to have pity on the victim, as might happen in the main State enquiry centres.

The first person to be so 'convinced' and to confess his 'crimes' was the former owner of the building, a well-known wine grower. In his own well-stocked cellars he wrote his confession in less than twenty-four hours.

Those few words of introduction were the only civilised statements I heard in that office. The abuse and tortures which followed are certainly written in the Book of Life and will be requited at the Last Judgement. I pray that God will give me the power to forgive those who have committed such atrocities against so many innocent people, and against myself.

Those who have escaped from such hell can tell stories that will seem unbelievable to many. For the free world the chapter of human cruelty closed with the defeat of Hitler. Other Westerners will prefer not to hear: the war was enough.

There are those, however, who know the real state of affairs. They know that in Communist countries there are thousands of prisons, concentration camps, psychiatric asylums. Will they believe if I dare to tell them that despite the 'tests' I underwent, my soul remained at peace, always close to heaven through prayer, and quite undisturbed? That while I submitted resignedly to physical torture my spiritual nature, detached from the flesh, rejoiced in my suffering?

After five days of unbroken investigation and 'tests', the enquiry took a dangerous turn. The slightest allusion to another prisoner in my dossier, the least sign of fear would have encouraged my torturers to redouble their efforts to get my confession. If I reached that crucial point I would be quite unable to defend myself. On the contrary, I would embroil many other people who, I hoped, had not been discovered and imprisoned. In these circumstances the power of prayer was extraordinary – and miraculous.

The questions had followed a logical sequence from the start of the enquiry. Though I turned them aside, each day my inquisitors got closer to the heart of the matter. It was only to be expected that any reasonable being would ask me – and concentrate upon – one key question: I anticipated the moment with terror. It seemed quite unavoidable. I held my breath. It didn't come. It never came. This was the first miracle of that extraordinary Christmas.

None of the 'gentlemen' who interrogated me – whether all together or in teams, never less than two at a time – none of them asked me this question, though it was the next logical step, and must have been implied by my whole dossier.

I felt sure that Someone unseen was keeping close to me, and intervening each time my enemies had to be misled. I felt – could almost touch – the presence of my guardian angel. He was there to throw spanners in their works, to cloud their reasoning so that they failed to ask the one question which would have led to the imprisonment of many innocent people, whose only guilt was that of refusing to bow down before totalitarian, atheistic Communism.

For the next twenty-four hours they failed to broach the crucial subject. I grew confident that God would not allow my enemies to proceed too far with their researches, despite all their efforts. He would not allow them to imprison others.

On the morning of December 24th, when I was led back to the office after all too brief a rest, perched on the edge of my bed (not permitted to sleep, and under a guard's surveillance), I was unpleasantly surprised by the sight of five officers sitting at their table. They ordered me to stay on my feet, despite my obvious fatigue, and taking advantage of my weakened state harrassed me with a hail of questions. They went right back over the whole investigation, punctuating their demands with foul insults and hideous threats.

After four hours of this my heart suddenly missed a beat. 'This is it,' I thought. The colonel stopped the interrogation and circulated my dossier to each officer after opening it to a page near the end. Each of them studied it carefully.

I was sure that the key question was written there in huge letters. It was all over . . . but no. After examining the page and discussing it, one of the officers left the room, while the others began to fling the same old questions at me once more. The danger receded. I felt such a wave of relief that I couldn't help laughing out loud. My tormentors seemed so ridiculous in their bewilderment, they were so small and silly! I went on laughing, laughing, laughing . . .

'Take her downstairs,' the colonel told his adjutant. 'Leave her asleep till tomorrow. If the attack continues, let me know.'

The cellar's silence no longer seemed depressing: it had become solemn, and friendly. My solitude that night helped me to become more fully aware of the overwhelming Christian event we celebrate at Christmas.

The strange Christmas night I spent in that cellar was truly gentle and calm. No window looked out into the night, but the star of Bethlehem shone brightly in my heart, and there I knew the mystery of the birth of Jesus. Within my soul was the crib, the baby Jesus, and there too were His parents, the angels, the three Kings – and, among them all, my parents and my friends.

Jesus *lived* within me. My whole being was full of His presence. The star's light shone more strongly, and the joy I felt at belonging to Jesus grew stronger too – much too strong for my poor heart. Christmas carols soared marvellously about me: the skies opened, flooding my cell with song, colour and delight.

'Lord Jesus!' I cried suddenly, hiding my face in my hands. 'I can't take it! Your blessing is too great for me – for an insignificant creature like me! Your light is too bright for me to bear!'

A few seconds later I looked around. The calm, quiet, atmosphere of the cellar surrounded me. 'Jesus was here on Christmas night,' I murmured to myself.

That was the most wonderful Christmas I have ever had. All the same, I shall always regret that I did not let myself be transported utterly in the ecstasy of the Holy Night.

* * *

After Christmas the enquiry resumed its unchanging rhythm, night after night with the same strange, mysterious quality – hidden away in a single-storey villa where I was quite alone with my inquisitors and a handful of guards. The guards kept watch on me during the day and the others took charge of me at night.

One evening, something like two weeks after my arrival at the villa, during which time not a soul had been imprisoned in the other cellars, I entered the office as usual to find only two of the three investigators who had been working on my case to that point.

I sat down and waited for the interrogation to begin, with its usual procedures and special ritual.

The two officers seemed ready to begin. Deep in my file, they did not say a word. I took the opportunity to recite my favourite psalm and to pray urgently that God would keep me safe from all harm.

Suddenly the door swung open to admit a tall man, brown-haired, with a haughty manner and unpleasantly thick eyebrows. He burst in like a meteor, briskly removed his black jacket, sat down between the other two and said:

'Listen to me, my girl. For more than three years now you've been playing with us. This enquiry interests us particularly deeply, but ever since your arrest you've led all our investigators right up the garden path. We started the enquiry again, both where you were working and at the Ministry, and you've kept on wasting our time with the same nonsense. Because of you we've been taken to task by our superiors, who are anxious to close the case and bring the guilty parties to justice. You've been here for two weeks now under constant questioning by competent men. Even here in this house where you know perfectly well that we're not accountable for the methods we use to get at the truth – even in a house which you could very well leave feet first, with no guilt on our hands – you have failed to answer us with the kind of sincerity which would allow us to close your file once and for all. You've lied to us from first to last. We've used every method we thought necessary to make you talk, but you have a peculiar gift for misleading the most experienced investigators.

'Now look. I know your case in every detail, and this is what I've decided to do. We're going to scrap everything that has been said and written up to this point. Understand? We're going to destroy hundreds of pages which have cost us effort and you suffering. We're wiping out everything that's gone before. From Monday (it was now Friday) we'll start the enquiry again from the beginning. I will conduct it personally together with other comrades. You will do your best to make our work easy and you'll cut out all your little tales, and it'll be that much better for you and for us. If you refuse, we'll keep you here and use the most modern 'treatments' in earnest to help you regain your memory, until you can even recall the milk you sucked at your mother's breast . . . It's your own choice!'

He then turned to his companions.

'Comrades, I'd like to thank you for all the hard work you've done. From Monday my team will take over. The current files will be scrapped, and starting next week we'll build up a file of some real value. You may go.'

I suddenly felt the urge to speak to this unknown officer, while his 'comrades' were collecting their papers together and preparing to leave.

'Colonel, I'd like to talk to you for a few moments. May I?'

'Why not? Go ahead.'

'You've talked about a file that is a pack of lies, and about getting other statements to build up a file closer to the truth. I completely understand everything you've said tonight. Humanly speaking, I'm in your hands and I've got no way of going against your decisions. I'd only like to point out that I have nothing to add to what I've said up till now, and that nothing whatsoever can make me say something different. If certain parts of my life seem obscure to you, what makes you think that they were controlled from outside and not determined by my own initiative? Why ask yourselves questions that range far beyond my intentions and actions? I believe that an investigator should be a good psychologist above everything else: he needs to have the imagination of a writer, the understanding of a priest and the patience of a psychiatrist. And if you've studied my poor self in this way, you will have quickly understood that I've been telling the truth and that the 'activities' I spoke of when they were raised certainly do not deserve the kind of attention you've given them – to the point of spending night after night, together with your superiors and junior officers, not to mention heaven knows how many meetings and other efforts.'

'What are you up to now? I don't understand a thing you're saying. What I've decided is what goes. That's all there is to say!'

'I'm not going against your decisions at all, as I've already told you. I'm only trying to help you. If you don't know the way someone's mind works – their character – then you can't say that you've really studied them.'

'Look, we're not here to conduct a psychiatric examination, but to direct an enquiry. Got it?'

'Yes, I understand perfectly well. But that's the point: if your enquiry is going to succeed, what I'm saying is highly relevant.'

'When your party gets back to power and you lead investigations into our activites, you can put your theories into practice . . .'

'I don't expect my party to get back to power. And even if it did I wouldn't participate in this kind of affair for anything in the world.'

'We really appreciate the scorn you pour on our work.'

'I'm not trying to be scornful at all. I've always tried, and I'll go on trying, never to look down on any of my fellow creatures. If I've angered you, Colonel, please believe that as a Christian I do my utmost to love all men, even those who cause me suffering . . .'

'I can assure you we don't need your love!'

'We all need love, the love which only God can produce in the souls of His creatures.'

'Forget it,' said the colonel. 'I've told you my decision. You can think about it till Monday. If you don't co-operate, I disclaim all responsibility for what happens to you.'

He rang, and the guard led me away, blindfolded, to my cellar.

* * *

Many years have passed, but the hours I spent after this conversation are as clear in my memory as if they were yesterday. I have endured a good deal of suffering in the course of different enquiries, but with God's support I was able to stand firm and to keep my reason. However, with the prospect of this 'new system' of investigation it was obvious to me that these men were going to give me injections which would destroy all my resistance.

I have to admit that my inner peace was not all that it might have been during the next two days. My feelings swung back and forth so rapidly that by the Sunday evening, as I prayed before falling asleep, I was thoroughly ashamed to admit that fear was deeply rooted in my heart and that such peace as I had was far from profound.

I slept uneasily, between peace and unrest, confidence and anxiety. I could only be sure of one thing: that I must remain in total submission to the will of the Almighty – though I was unable to contemplate the events of the following day with complete trust and acceptance.

I woke at dawn rested and in a better frame of mind. I had had a beautiful dream, and when I awoke I was still under its spell. I relived it, closing my eyes to sleep again and return to it. I couldn't tell whether I was dreaming once more or piecing together what I had seen. I had the pleasant impression that I was flying, leaving the prison – that I was back in the house where I had lived as child and adolescent, where I had spent the happiest times of my life. I was in our sitting-room, where beside my concert piano stood the harmonium father had given my mother. She would spend hours at a time at this instrument, playing religious pieces and accompanying Alice's mother, her old friend, who shared her faith and had a fine voice. During my adolescence, I found they made far too much fuss about their religion: people laughed at them, all the more because they were both intellectuals and belonged to the best society. At school Alice and I had to tolerate nasty comments from our classmates and teachers on the exaggerated mysticism of our mothers. That was why we did everything we could to free ourselves from our faiths and to give the impression that our convictions were quite different.

Mother's harmonium used to be covered with a laquered cloth on which she had written in French, in large letters: 'He saved me because He loves me.' I frequently found myself irritated beyond measure by the cloth, always draped across the instrument. When I brought friends and classmates home, I would snatch off the harmonium cover and screw it up in a drawer. I was ashamed of it. Mother's faith made me blush: I would have liked to be the same as the rest of my gang, who were quite indifferent to religious problems and tended to be sarcastic about anything to do with mysticism.

Mother used to look at me reproachfully. Each time she would comment, 'One day you'll be sorry for all this.'

As I hung between dream and reality I saw once again, for the first time in many years, the harmonium and its brightly coloured cloth in the corner of the sitting-room. So much had happened to me that I had completely forgotten my earlier reprehensible behaviour. Though the dream brought back to me yet another blameworthy aspect of my past, I was not utterly cast down as had often been the case when I remembered some past sin. On the contrary, I wanted to remain half asleep, savouring in my mind that corner, the words on the cloth and the happiness which accompanied the dream.

Slowly it faded away: I rubbed my eyes, woke up and recognised that the fatal day was upon me. However, nothing could disturb my peace of mind; I was tranquil, utterly calm, while in my mind I saw the words on the harmonium, the large, brightly painted letters.

Every vestige of fear had passed.

I washed and prayed, but strangely did not ask God to protect me from the trials ahead.

The day passed quickly enough. My dream behind me, I quietly relived a number of memories from my childhood, calling to mind well-loved faces I remembered: former friends at school, my family.

That night I felt neither anxiety nor anguish. I repeated the words I had seen that morning. I constantly found my mind returning to the sitting-room which had enchanted me in the dream.

No one called me for interrogation that night.

The next day I was also left in peace.

On the third day the guard entered.

'Come with me and have a bath.'

This seemed strange, but I followed him obediently. According to him it was ten o'clock in the morning. I calmly had a bath, and as I was going into the bathroom he whispered: 'Make the most of it, have a good wash. You'll be going back to work tomorrow. I'll warn you before they arrive, so that they don't surprise you in your cell. But watch out, don't say a thing!'

Everything happened just as the guard had said.

On Thursday morning he came and shook me gently.

'Wake up, but pretend you're still asleep. It's four o'clock. They'll come and get you in thirty minutes. It's better for you to be awake so that you're not afraid: there'll be quite a few of them.'

'How can I ever thank you?'

'Don't worry about that. You know, there are still some decent people on our side . . .'

As the guard had said, about half an hour later five men, each as unpleasant as the next, burst into the room.

'That's the one?'

'Yes, that's her. Grab her and take her along.'

Goggles, stairs, corridors . . . ultimately I smelt the fresh morning air. In the car I was driven yet again towards some unknown destination. I hoped I was being taken back to work. It might also be some place specialising in 'new' forms of torture, which I had feared so much and which now left me utterly indifferent.

It was well on into the morning when my goggles were removed. We were on the road which separated the barracks from the pigsties. A warm glow of light flooded my heart: I was back among friends.

After the camp administration had taken charge of me at the gate, I entered my barracks as if I was coming home. It was cold and smelt nasty. What did that matter?

I flung myself down on my bed and closed my eyes, eager to thank Jesus for granting my prayers. But the verse mother had painted on the cloth kept coming to mind.

'He saved me because He loves me.'

It was only then I understood what had happened.

Jesus wanted to tell me through the dream that He had saved me from the questioning I had feared so much; that He had heard my prayer; that He had saved me because He loved me. This explained the sense of security that I had felt on waking and which had not left me since. That was why peace had returned to my heart after all those threats. That was why I felt able to entrust myself so calmly to His care.

I could scarcely prevent myself from leaping across the barracks for joy. I wanted to shout out loud with happiness. Such a prompt answer to my prayer – and moreover through words so utterly suited to my needs – filled me with rejoicing.

When I had calmed down a little and had thought further about the Lord's direct intervention, I smiled quietly. In His mercy He gave me His answer in a dream, I thought. He could have chosen any dream to warn me. But He chose precisely the words on the harmonium cover which I was so ashamed of and used to hide. He used such tremendous delicacy to reproach me for this past transgression, and incredible tact in telling me that He was wiping it out, as He has wiped out so many others.

A true friend. He had not wanted anything to trouble our friendship.

And although the phrase 'He saved me because He loves me' had meant nothing to my lost soul in the past, though I had grieved Him by blushing at His holy words, it was precisely through those same words that He told me that He had saved me from the terrible trial awaiting me, and at the very moment when I really knew His love.

* * *

As the snow and ice made it impossible to work in the fields, we were taken to Ghencea to wait for the weather to improve.

From the beginning of February, we were lodged in dark and miserable barracks. We were impossibly crowded, as large numbers of men and women from camps all over the area passed through Ghencea, which was the terminal for prisoners destined for labour camps, for transfer and for those who were 'hibernating'.

Thanks to past experience we were not frightened by the mass of people, the variety of different types, the foul language or the filth which pervaded the barracks. By dint of a number of 'wrinkles' which prisoners learn, we did our best to keep together as far as possible, and in general succeeded. We were delighted to find a number of old friends whom we had lost sight of as we travelled from one prison or camp to another. What was more, new prisoners, who had been recently arrested, were able to pass on more up-to-date political news. The range of people in whose company we spent those weeks ran from gipsy to princess, from the foulest criminal to the holiest religious. Though we were crammed in together on our beds, we were glad to be able to stretch out our weary bodies for a while and to talk freely. The guards at Ghencea only had outside duties, and the women warders would only intervene if there were fights among the ordinary prisoners or if the racket got impossibly loud.

One evening Lieutenant Craciun, of whom I had unpleasant memories, appeared with his guards and shouted: 'All those whose names I read out will be set free! They will get their belongings together and line up next to the door two by two. No noise, no kissing or hugging, no talking. Now pay attention!'

He then read out the list of names.

He had no problems in announcing the names of those who were to get their freedom: despite their joy, we all held our breath, gripped by intense emotion. The names came one after another as we stood rigid, waiting for our own.

When I heard 'Sabina Wurmbrand', I had the impression that mine would follow. I strained, trembling, to catch each name, but the list ended without mentioning me. I gave scarce attention to Bintzea's movements, and thus failed to observe what she did in the crucial moments before she left prison. I seemed to recall in the hours that followed that her face seemed to have lost the light that normally filled it: knowing that this was probably the final separation, Bintzea was undoubtedly sad not to have had even a smile as she left.

I was naturally delighted that a first batch of political prisoners had been released. I rejoiced – we all rejoiced over each one of them – but I was above all happy that Bintzea was returning to her home, where she was needed not only by her immediate family but also by a large number of believers for whom she represented a real blessing. I pictured her going from house to house, bringing to each one some uplifting thought and a word of encouragement. I was also sure that she would visit my parents as soon as she had kissed Michael and Alice. How surprised my mother and father would be when she suddenly appeared! It would strengthen their hope that I in turn would also return to them.

This event took on huge proportions as each excited group discussed it fervently. It was unique in the four years I had spent in prison. Each prisoner thought with renewed optimism about her own release.

'They're going to let us all go: there's a commission – attorneys are hard at work in the office . . .'

'We'll be leaving in groups of twenty to thirty just like this evening . . .'

It was late at night before the barracks grew quiet and a refreshing sleep calmed our tense emotions.

When I awoke the next morning, without Bintzea beside me, I finally believed that the group's departure was no dream, but glorious reality.

I waited quietly for reveille, when everyone had to scramble down off their bunks for roll call. The officers were always late in calling the roll, but we had to await them standing up.

In my group they were excitedly discussing the events of the day before.

'They'll still be asleep. They must have got to bed very late, as they'll have been telling their families all about it . . .'

'Think of all the good things they'll have been eating.'

'Yes! This morning they'll drink coffee with fresh bread, butter, jam . . .'

'They'll be able to take a real hot bath . . .'

'They'll be able to put on comfortable clothes. It must be

so lovely to wear silk stockings and good shoes.'

Everyone had a touch of envy in their voices, but above all they were happy.

'You talk away like that,' commented one old woman, 'but you don't ask where the coffee and butter and jam are coming from. Do you think that you've only to clap your hands and they'll be there for the taking? Have you forgotten how worried you were when you got food parcels from home and wondered how much they cost your families?'

'She's right,' said a girl who had been recently arrested. 'You've no idea of the misery we've suffered everywhere. As for hot baths, in most houses with central heating they only have hot water twice a week. The situation isn't that wonderful. Not to mention the homes which are still using wood or coal.'

'Whatever the case, they're still free, and that's what counts.'

After listening to the comments from this group, I moved on to another circle nearby, composed of a mixture of new prisoners and old-timers. Some I knew well, others less so. The same kind of discussion was also under way here.

The women's faces were sad: they were missing their children, their parents, their husband or fiancé. The previous day's departure had thrown them into turmoil. What was more, the weather was cloudy and though the lights were on, the barracks remained dark and gloomy.

Some of the women fasted on Fridays, and today was a Friday. To cheer them a little I suggested:

'It's Friday, and several of you are fasting. What would you think of starting the day with a psalm? Would you like to?'

'Oh, yes,' they chorused – even those who did not share our faith.

'In that case I'll recite Psalm 91 to you.'

When I reached the fifth verse Eva Hecht, who was with us, stopped me suddenly and said, blushing, with a quaver in her voice:

'Forgive me for interrupting you, but it's so beautiful! Will you let me recite the rest?'

I hesitated, as I did not know whether she had any religious inclinations: we had exchanged very few words, as she was a withdrawn and solitary person. But I stepped aside for her. Eva began:

> Thou shalt not be afraid for the terror by night; nor
> for the arrow that flieth by day;
> Nor for the pestilence that walketh in darkness; nor
> for the destruction that wasteth at noonday . . .

She went right through to the end of this extraordinary psalm, her voice growing more and more fervent as she reached the end:

> Because he hath set his love upon me, therefore will I
> deliver him: I will set him on high, because he hath
> known my name.
> He shall call upon me, and I will answer him: I will be
> with him in trouble; I will deliver him, and honour
> him.
> With long life will I satisfy him, and shew him my
> salvation.

She paused for a moment, then said to us, her face shining:

'Since Nicole began this psalm, I'll tell you how I know it and all that it represents for me. I spent more than a year in solitary confinement. During this whole time, almost every night I was interrogated under a blinding light. I was tortured, and had reached the end of my tether. The enquiry was quite pointless – they wanted to make me confess what I hadn't done, because to tell you the truth politics have never really interested me. My interrogators had reduced me to a bunch of rags: they were merely bent on tormenting me. I feared them so much that when I stood before them I trembled like a leaf and would beg them either to leave me alone or to kill me. I had almost lost my sight because of the projector they used to blind me with each night. I could feel myself losing my sanity. I tried to bite open my veins several times, but I didn't succeed in dying. Each time I was carried off to the infirmary, the doctor and his assistants would mock me, and ask, "Do you really think it's so easy to die? Here death only comes when you've confessed everything. Remember, confession first . . ."

'When I was back on my feet and the questioning began again, the interrogators would poke fun at me. "So who got you to criticise our comrade Minister of the Interior? You went into the market-place and told everyone that he used to organise orgies with colleagues on the Central Committee, and that the next morning, dead drunk, they would indulge in their favourite game, pelting one another with oranges . . ."

'I would admit it.

'"Yes, I agree that I said that. Look, I'm only a woman, and I've lived most of my life with women, and everyone knows that we like to gossip . . ."

'"All right. You've also lived for a good deal of the time among men, or rather with men," they would add to irritate me.

'"Everyone's free to live their life as they want to . . . You have no reason to aggravate me. Yes, I've had boy-friends, but none of them were spies, as you want me to say."

'"Every one of them was bourgeois through and through, and they were all in the pay of the Americans. We want you to tell us about the contacts each of them had with the American agents. Otherwise you'll never get out of here."

'When I was able to speak, I tried my best to exonerate myself.

'"Do you think that a real spy would give secrets away to a girl-friend? I doubt if he would even let his wife know."

'"We're not talking about major secrets. But you know

all about their contacts, their friendships, the people they met."

'"I would have known about them if I had kept in touch over the last few years with friends from my past. But I'd completely broken with them. I loved one man and saw only him."

'"Didn't you have any adventures, then, when you went to the soirées held by Teohari Georgescu and he enjoyed himself so much?" (Georgescu was formerly the Minister of the Interior.) "And when you went to Western embassies, or when the ladies from those embassies came to you, did you never get the chance to talk with them, to find something special to tell them?"

'That was how they used to torment me night after night,' Eva continued. 'You see, I used to be a fashion designer, as some of you may know. My customers were from the highest strata of society. Thanks to my establishment's reputation, my clients were the richest women and the spouses of the diplomats of Bucharest. When the Communists gained power, I was invited to work for the top-ranking Communist ladies. One faithful client was Mrs. Teohari Georgescu. She was very pretentious, a real coquette, and at one point she considered me quite indispensable. She often asked me to visit her house, and this gave me the opportunity to see how people lived in such a palace – the owner had been sent packing, to work for his living. I attended several receptions, and was scared by the orgies that used to take place at the end. Unfortunately I was weak enough to tell stories about what I had seen there. I told my family and friends, who were so poor they had to queue for bread or a few scraps of meat. At Teohari's I saw nothing but oranges, chocolate, and all sorts of delicacies.

'My remarks must have reached the ears of the people concerned, and to silence me they had me arrested. During the enquiry I acknowledged that I had been indiscreet, but my stories had been no more than a gesture against the injustice and privilege so evident among those who claimed to be friends of the people . . .'

'They must have really thrashed you, if you told them that!' said a girl.

'Of course they did . . . after raining blows on me they began the investigation I mentioned. They scrutinised my whole life and examined all the friends and acquaintances I could have had. Some of these had left for the West, others mouldered in prison, and yet others were still free. They tortured me for nearly a year, as I told you, to make me confess that all of them were spies in the pay of the Americans. They even wanted to make me say that I was the one who established the contacts between most of them and the foreign powers, probably when I visited the embassies where I had clients.'

'It's horrible,' said a voice. 'What a ghastly situation!'

I watched Eva Hecht without understanding why she was suddenly opening out to us like this: she was usually content to say good morning or give just a gracious smile. I had tried to get closer to her under various pretexts, but without success. I didn't understand her motives for describing her case and the purpose of her interrogation in such detail, especially as that was specifically forbidden. And why, above all, had she chosen to do so to a group in which every woman was a stranger to her? They waited with keen interest for Eva to take up her tale once again.

I too was fascinated by her words, and visualised her in her former context: a beautiful distinguished woman wearing dresses every bit as sumptuous as the finest she had created for others. Today she was nothing but a vague shadow from a past rich in gratification of the senses and in passing illusions.

Officer Craciun and his guard at last appeared to call the roll. He made disparaging remarks about the cleanliness of the barracks, swore at us and departed majestically with his contingent.

The circle around Eva automatically came together again. Everyone waited for her to continue her story.

Eva, however, seemed embarrassed at having said so much. I realised that she was regretting what she had told us about the enquiry, and seemed worried.

'Eva,' I said to help her along, 'you interrupted me as I was reciting that psalm. Everything you've said was very interesting, but explain to us why you wanted so badly to recite it yourself. How did you know it by heart?'

Eva took a deep breath.

'I didn't give you that digression on my sufferings for nothing. I wanted you to understand what a desperate state I was in after hundreds of nights of interrogation.'

'But how did you get out of it?' interrupted one woman, curious and upset by all she'd heard.

'I didn't exactly get out of it,' replied Eva with a gentle smile. 'In fact it was a real miracle . . .

'One morning the sun shone down into my cell. I couldn't stand it, as my eyes were too tired. To protect myself from its beams I turned my face to the wall, my hand shading my eyes. It frightened me that I couldn't even take the sun's health-giving light any longer. I thought I must have something seriously wrong with my eyes. Suddenly, as I went on staring at the wall, I thought I could make out letters scratched onto the surface. At first I thought it was just a hallucination brought on by my damaged eyes. Then I looked harder and began reading – reading! The first words I read were those Nicole has just quoted. The inscription broke off at the point where I interrupted. But when I examined the wall more closely, I saw that after the phrase I mentioned there was an arrow which showed where the text continued. Here I found the section I recited to you. Following on along the arrow I came to a kind of explanation by the person who had written down the psalm on three of the four walls. After each text there was a commentary. I say "the person" because as I studied the words at length from that day onwards I noticed that they were all in the same handwriting and followed the same thought patterns.

'That was how I came to read the psalm, and began to understand deep down inside the real cause of my sufferings during the past year or more – quite a different cause from the one the interrogators wanted me to admit. I was reaping the reward for the flighty life I used to lead. It was my own sins which had led me into this predicament. It had never occurred to me before that I did not have the right to order my life and other people's just as I pleased; but in my cell I discovered how true that was. I had never once prayed to God to ask His forgiveness or His help. It was then I understood that in order to learn to pray in truth, I needed the police to hold me in just such a ghastly situation. I read right through that day without stopping, searching out everything I could find on the walls. As I thought seriously about the matters I had just discovered, I reached the logical conclusion that I was a sinner and that I needed God's forgiveness. But to obtain forgiveness I had to repent of everything which marred my past and make a solemn resolution never to adopt again the life which I had led before my arrest. Without a moment's hesitation, using the words which came to my lips and inspired by the lines I had found scrawled on the walls, I spoke to God, and opened my heart to Him with all its corruption. I asked Him to forgive me, to guide me, to protect me. I prayed that He would help me to escape from the inquisitors' clutches and promised Him that once I was free, if that was His will, my life would take a radically new course.

'At once a sense of peace stole over me. I had the impression that the One who is goodness itself touched my forehead with His hand, wiping away the lines there. I turned towards the skylight through which the sun had shone. The sun had gone, but on the other hand my heart had been utterly and permanently transformed.'

'How mysterious are Your ways, O Lord!' murmured Stella. 'What an incredible tale . . . it seems quite fantastic.'

Eva was still deep in her story.

'That same evening I walked in and stood before the investigators as though I was supported at every step. I stood upright and I wasn't crying any longer, because I was resting on the presence of God in my heart and thoughts. I knew that I was no longer alone and that I was living under the shadow of the Almighty. When they turned their reflector full into my eyes I didn't wince, and when they began their questions and torments I did not weep, nor beg them to let me die rather than suffer so.

'One of the interrogators was struck by my attitude and asked me suspiciously, "What is the matter with you?"

'"Nothing," I replied calmly.

'"Have you been in touch with anyone? Have you spoken to anyone?" He supposed, doubtless, that I had managed to get in touch with somebody outside by bribing one of the guards. Perhaps I had discovered something – for example, that Teohari Georgescu himself was a prisoner in the cellars of the Ministry of the Interior, though he had once been its head.

'"Yes," I replied. "I've been talking to God."

'That answer was enough to get me sent straight back to my cell.

'After that evening I continued to scrutinise my past and to draw closer to the things of the spirit. The interrogators found they were dealing with someone completely different. Poor men, in their spiritual poverty they quite failed to understand: they only knew that my mental anguish was at an end and that they couldn't get a thing out of me. They sent for me more and more rarely, reckoned I was ill, and less than a month after I had told them that I had spoken with God, which was nothing other than the truth, they had me transferred to the Ferma Rosia, where I met a number of you.'

'What an amazing story,' muttered several of her audience, deeply impressed.

The rest of us stayed silent, acknowledging the impact of Eva's confession.

With a distant look in her eyes Eva took up the account once more:

'Since that glorious morning when I found the writing on the walls of my cell, I've been cherishing the hope that one day, when our country is really free, I will be able to put my plan into effect. I want to insert notices in the papers looking for the person who was confined in a cell at Malmaison Prison and, despite the risks, scratched what amounted to a course in the Bible and extracts from the Scriptures on the walls – requesting that they get in touch with me. I'm convinced that I'll find her. I've got one sister, whom I love dearly, but the person who wrote on the walls of that cell in Malmaison prison will be a sister or brother dearer to me than my family. I will love them with all the love of the new spirit within me, because it's thanks to them that I've changed so much; I owe them my life, my sight, my sanity and above all the fact that I've found my spiritual self. When I meet that person I'll clasp them in my arms, then kiss their feet. No one will ever separate us.'

As everyone was looking at Eva, no one noticed that my face was streaming with tears.

'Eva –' my voice was choked with sobs. 'You were in cell Twenty-four at Malmaison Prison. You don't need to put an advert in the papers, because the person whom you can consider your sister from now on is standing right in front of you. I wrote the words you've been telling us about: I did it to help those who were suffering as you have suffered. God called you to Himself thanks to the scrawls I did with a prune stone. It is one more proof that He has heard my fervent prayers.'

We stumbled into each other's arms and wept for a long time. All of those who had been present during Eva's tale and my reply wept with us, shedding many tears.

From that day on Eva and I were inseparable. Right through our imprisonment and later, when we were released, a strong bond united us.

The story of her life spoke so powerfully to me that one day I hope to write it fully for others to read. Eva is no longer in this world, but she is certainly with all those who through their sufferings responded to God's call, and now rest in peace.

* * *

One morning at Ghencea we learnt that Stalin was dead. The news spread like wildfire: the women grew more and more excited as they saw in the event some reason to hope that they might be freed. I couldn't share in the general rejoicing: I was simply convinced that my fate was in the Lord's hands.

At the end of March we were sent out to work in the fields once more. This time we were despatched to Bragadiru Farm, the farm from which I had managed to rescue Bintzea.

Because of the cold, the work was particularly hard, and the pace got faster and faster. But I wouldn't let myself join the complaining that arose on all sides. Through prayer I managed to cope with my tasks, fortified by the certainty that God asks nothing that is beyond the strength of those that trust in Him. I did my best to get this truth through to the dear companions who shared my suffering, and I used to interrupt them as soon as they began, 'But I can't . . .'

One evening I was taken from Bragadiru with twenty or so women whom the authorities reckoned the most dangerous, and we were sent to Targsor prison. The International Youth Festival in Bucharest was in preparation, and those responsible for the work camps were afraid that one or another of the young people taking part would get the idea of taking a trip out of town. Our farm was right beside the main road, so the twenty of us who knew foreign languages might be discovered and 'interviewed' by the tourists. There was a chance that in talking to us they might learn that we were not common criminals but rather political prisoners, which would not have suited the regime at all. That was why we were placed under cover at Targsor.

Like Mislea, Targsor was a former monastery which had been converted into a work camp. Prison uniforms were made there. In view of the number of prisoners and the ever-increasing demand, the work now continued right around the clock, with three teams. The norms were beyond belief. If you broke a needle, or your machine failed, the penalty was twenty-four hours in your cell without food. It was nearly impossible not to break your needle on the over-thick cloth, using machines which had not been designed for such work.

'Who knows how much wheat we had to give the Soviets for such rejects?' commented one friend.

She was right. But we were exploited to the very limits of our strength, and could do nothing about it.

Together with Eva, Ecaterina, Marioana and Cella, not to forget the other dear friends with us in Targsor, we did our best to resist the punishing routine. Though we would be weary and starving after eight hours' work, we were not even allowed to sleep. When we were on the night shift, we would return to the dormitory to rest, only to be kept wide awake by the row from the women who had been at work the previous afternoon and had been able to sleep during the night.

The problem was that though we had been separated from the ordinary prisoners we now shared the dormitory with thieves and criminals. This meant a continuous uproar. To make life still more unpleasant, the female warders used to drag out the miseries of the afternoon by requiring us to clean the place each day. This meant that we had to tug the mattresses and bedsteads out into the yard each afternoon. We would pile them on the ground, sweep the room, splash the iron beds with fuel, then put everything back in its place for the evening team's return. Clouds of dust arose when we beat the mattresses with our hands (we had nothing else to beat them with), and mingled with the dust already in the yard. The work was bad enough, but it made it far worse to be expected to sleep on such beds. We were so bone-tired, however, that we would have relished the chance to sleep – if we'd been given time. But once the cleaning was over the meal was served, and then we had to go back to the workshops if we were on the night shift.

Our stay at Targsor was an absolute hell. As we laboured through the night we would often find ourselves dozing off, but the director kept watch on us – or appointed someone in his stead – through the large windows which looked out over the workshop yard. If anyone was caught sleeping, they were despatched immediately to the 'black hole'. We therefore kept a permanent eye on one another, shaking ourselves awake, doing our best to avoid the horrors of the punishment cell. Our bodies were weak after so many years of varied suffering: our nerves were shot to pieces after torture, interrogation and labour camps.

For most of the women our stay in Targsor passed slowly and painfully. For those of us who had faith, it was yet another form of suffering to see them sink obstinately into the despair which aggravated the burden of their imprisonment.

One night in August it was my turn to fetch the material from the store. I crossed the yard some way ahead of the guard, and as I returned towards the workshop with a sack of cloth in my arms, I had to tilt my head back (the sack came up to my chin). I looked up at the sky, which was dark blue and spangled with stars. As I searched the vault of heaven with my gaze I suddenly heard myself sighing, without realising it, 'Oh, Father, I just can't take any more!' Just at that moment a shooting star fell.

I took my place at the sewing machine once more and tried mentally to scold myself for having uttered the words that I had formally forbidden myself to use during my first days in prison. I had always avoided them in both speech and thought. And now they slip out when you aren't paying attention! I chided myself. My mind flung accusations at me, but curiously my spirit remained at peace, without a shadow of guilt or sadness. I spent the rest of the night trying to analyse what had happened; I wanted to know why my soul was so much at peace while my mind was so keen to condemn. I pictured the glowing sky once again and visualised the bright ribbon of the shooting star.

Something told me that I had experienced something exceptional, perhaps crucial. I felt that the words had come to my lips spontaneously, that I had said them without thinking about them. It was as if a voice inside was telling me that I was coming towards some kind of ending.

A few days later, as I entered the workshop, I heard a guard calling my name.

'Leave all that: go to the dormitory and get your things.'

I exchanged glances with Ecaterina, the only person to whom I had mentioned what worried me on the night the star fell. Then I followed the guard.

Though it was night, I was still required to wear the goggles for the journey to Bucharest. I was in a jeep with three men, including the driver. I was so weary that after murmuring the Lord's Prayer I fell asleep and only woke when we reached a massive gate. This opened, and immediately afterwards I felt us going up a slope. I was back in the Malmaison once more.

I was shut in my cell in accordance with the old ritual I have described. Without waiting for permission to lie down, I flung myself on the bunk and continued to sleep soundly. The next day was a Sunday, and I awoke with a sense of freedom and lightness. Was it a presentiment of happiness to come?

On Monday morning, to my astonishment, the guard led me up to an office. It was just on ten o'clock. An officer whom I had never seen received me and invited me to sit down. Two other officers came in. I didn't understand a thing, and their first question was:

'That dress you're wearing, is it the only one you've got?'

'Yes, I haven't had a parcel from home for a long time.'

'It's badly torn and very poorly mended.'

'Yes, I know, but I haven't had the means of doing a better job.'

Then the interrogation began, right from the start, right from the first page of the dossier which the colonel had told me would be destroyed.

I was called each morning and evening; but I got the impression that they were concerned merely to undertake a general revision of the file. I was asked the same questions and gave the same replies. With a few exceptions, none of the investigators took any of the questions further.

When I was alone in my cell again I didn't know what to think. Something was certainly in the wind. Were they checking the details of my dossier in preparation for a trial? The sequence of questions was different from preceding enquiries, but perhaps they would be satisfied with presenting the file to the court as it was, adding their own accusations or those of some third party; ultimately I would be sentenced indefinitely and sent for heaven knew how long to some prison or labour camp. The thought of a coming condemnation did not worry me.

I was interrogated for two weeks. Then no one paid any attention to me for a further fortnight. I was given excellent, even mouth-watering food. I put on weight, and my weakness disappeared along with my splitting headaches. The doctor came to see me twice a week and gave me medicines to build up my strength. There was a complete, continuing silence in my corridor. I could hear none of the usual protests or screams which had been so much a feature of previous interrogations. I got the impression that the neighbouring cells were empty: it looked as if I was in a privileged position. There was even an alcove with a shower in my cell, which I used each day.

'It's too good to last,' I told myself. 'They're just fattening me up, getting me into condition to display me at the trial.'

* * *

On September 24th I was taken to the office once more. When they removed my goggles there were six officers in front of me. Two were the ones who had started inquiring into my case in 1949.

The colonel whom I had faced then looked at me and told me solemnly, 'We've got some good news for you. You will be freed today.'

Everything began to turn before my eyes, but I tried to hold up. They noticed my sudden pallor.

'What's the matter? Are you ill? Do you find the news surprising?'

'What do you think? It's the first good news I've had since my arrest.'

'That's no reason to faint. You have always claimed you were innocent. That you are being freed now is no more than a result of your innocence,' he concluded, smiling ironically.

'Certainly I always expected this outcome. But you must appreciate that after four years of imprisonment the information that I'm to be freed comes as something of a shock.'

'We have always told you that as soon as we were able to establish your innocence you would be released.'

'Allow me to point out that you needed a good deal of time to reach that conclusion.'

'Just a moment,' a major broke in. 'We haven't reached that conclusion yet. We simply haven't been able to prove that you are guilty. That's why we're letting you go. But if in the future we get evidence against you then you'll be back with us.'

'In that case I've nothing to worry about.'

'Who can tell? As we see it, either you are really innocent and it's our fault for having kept you, or you have confounded everything so cleverly that you've been leading us a merry dance. Time alone will show which is the correct hypothesis. In the meantime, we can tell you that you will be taken home this evening, after dinner.'

Then they fired a stream of questions at me. Each in turn would take the file, leaf through it and ask something at random. I saw what they were doing: they wanted to check my statements while I was in this highly emotional state. They were just waiting for me to make a mistake while flustered by the thought of my approaching liberty.

However, I did not stray from my usual replies, though they harrassed me for more than two hours. There was no connection between the rapid questions, and I had to face first one officer then swing round and answer another. They were after some kind of return for their efforts right up to the last moment. I had to sign a paper saying that I would tell no one about the subject of my enquiry, nor the names of those who had interrogated me. I signed. They asked which address I expected to stay at. I gave my uncle's address, which was where my parents had been staying for years. Then I returned to the cell with the promise that at six that evening I would be set down at their door.

Time passed horribly slowly. I remained quite dumbfounded, unsure whether it was real or whether I was dreaming. I even held my head under the cold tap to try and come down to earth, because I felt as though I was floating and had lost all control over myself. I paced the cell, weeping and laughing for joy. I gave thanks to God, then suddenly imagined meeting my parents. I felt myself to see if I was really alive. I wondered whether I was really on my feet, whether I wasn't dreaming – as had happened to me so often during the previous years, when in my reveries I would be on the point of being released, or reunited with my family. But this time it was completely real, so real that my happiness bubbled over into joy.

In suspense I waited as the hours, the minutes, the seconds ticked by until the stupendous moment when the prison gates would open wide.

At last it came. I thanked God.

After the evening meal the door opened and two guards came in. They too seemed in excellent humour: 'Time to go!' they announced as they came across. 'On your way to freedom and fortune!'

Of course, even now they did not forget to blindfold me, and did not remove my goggles until I reached the room to which I had been taken on my arrival four years earlier. On the table I found the handbag I had carried, with the various bits and pieces it had contained, together with a new blue dress which didn't belong to me.

'We've bought you a dress,' the officer on duty told me. 'You're not very presentable in the one you've got on. Put it on in the cloakroom next door.'

'Thank you,' I murmured, 'but you shouldn't have troubled. I'll find plenty of clothes at home.'

'You're not going home in that state.'

I donned the dress, but without pleasure. That was the first and last time I wore it.

Blindfolded once more, I was guided into a limousine. We rolled gently down the slope to the gate, then zigzagged through the whole town. Without the detours I would have been home in fifteen minutes, but the police are steeped in political rigmarole and mystery. Did they think I didn't know where I was? Perhaps. Whatever the case, all orders are carried out strictly and blindly in a Communist state.

'If you're really letting me go, why are you keeping these goggles on me?' I asked quietly. 'I can feel there are people about. I would have liked to see the street lights.'

'Everything in its turn,' replied the guard sitting beside me.

When we reached the very middle of the town, three minutes from my uncle's home, the goggles were finally removed. As my gaze swept across the lovely Boulevard de la République, I felt indeed that I was free.

My heart beat more and more fiercely as we approached the house. We stopped in front of it. The three men in the car wished me good luck: 'God go with you,' I replied firmly.

I can't remember if I said anything else, whether or not I annoyed them, but I had done my duty. It was only a step from the car to the door. I was going to see those I loved.

EPILOGUE

Life in 'free' society began, as far as I was concerned, with every problem returning political prisoners might expect.

I looked for work. Everywhere I was turned down on various pretexts which hid the real reason, the taint of prison that hung about me.

Someone suggested that I give piano lessons, and found me three pupils. To start work was tremendously welcome: it gave me wings to be able to earn my daily bread.

Then I met Sergiu Grossu, a former journalist, poet and writer, whom I had met in 1948 and had heard preach in an Orthodox church in Bucharest. He had interested me deeply as a man, and also on account of his clandestine activities: he was one of the leaders of the illegal movement known as the 'Army of the Lord'. We had been separated for years by my arrest, but now that I was free we met each other frequently, and it was soon clear we had fallen in love. Despite all kinds of practical problems, including the lack of any fixed abode, we were united for ever.

We celebrated our engagement in a little Orthodox monastery at the mountain resort of Sinaia, a former summer residence of the royal family.

The wedding was sadly overshadowed: my uncle was dying, and my father seriously ill. The religious ceremony was held in a small church near my parents' home, and an old acquaintance offered us hospitality for a while. Shortly after my uncle's death, my father also died: my mother went to live with a friend, and vacated on our behalf the room where she and my father had lived for so many bitter years after they had been evicted from our house.

Police oppression grew more severe, especially after certain events in Hungary. In 1958–9, the arrests began again, ushering in a new reign of terror. Persecution became fiercer overnight. There were shameless attacks on believers with the sanction of the highest ecclesiastical bodies, who collaborated with the regime.

They took men, women, teenagers. One night Sergiu was arrested. I was distraught, knowing precisely what it meant to fall into the clutches of the security forces.

One trial followed another. Believers and poor innocent folk who loved their country found themselves accused of the most hideous crimes, each worse than the last. Dossiers abounded denouncing people as counter-revolutionaries or spies in the pay of the imperialists. Many peasants accused of such 'crimes' were not even able to understand the indictments. The lawyers appointed on their behalf flung charges at them, and the public prosecutor called for sentences of more than twenty years.

In my husband's case the investigation and subsequent trial ended with a sentence of twelve years' hard labour.

However, from 1962 to 1964 the government ordered a general amnesty for all political prisoners in Rumania. As the first groups began to return the general rejoicing knew no limits. Someone was missing in almost every family. Relatives and friends beseiged the stations as line after interminable line of prisoners began to return to their families. The country went wild with joy. The prisons stood empty: some inmates had lain there since 1941, when Marshal Antonescu held power; others had been arrested in 1944–5. Mothers, wives, husbands, children clasped in their arms the shadows and twisted skeletons that had once been men and women.

My husband's return brought us happiness and hope, though after his release he had to take jobs far below the level that his university degrees might have obtained. He found it hard to adapt to work in which he had not the slightest interest; moreover, he was compelled to nurse his indifferent health, a result of the harsh years of slavery in the Danube delta, where the prisoners had been set to harvest reeds.

The amnesty had little effect on the religious freedom which the constitution specified. Sergiu, like any other believer, was banned from all religious meetings and activities. This made our life much harder, for my husband's deepest desire was to serve God openly, which was nearly impossible.

After a while we began to consider the possibility of leaving Rumania for freedom in the West. We had to wait several years, however, before we could clearly perceive God's will.

French friends who knew our wishes had tried on several occasions, in different ways, to help us obtain exit visas. At one point we grew discouraged by the evasions we received from the passport office, especially since many were getting passports in the years 1968–9.

During this period we began to tell ourselves that perhaps we should never be allowed to leave the country. A close friend, the only one in Rumania who knew what we had in mind, then suggested that I approach a rather strange lady who had relatives high in government service, and above all a 'friend' at passport control. At this point Rumania was enjoying a certain liberty, and it was usual to find all sorts of deals going on, including the buying and selling of 'influence'.

My conversation with this lady was brief and to the point. I explained the steps we had taken concerning our six-month visit to France (our official story!) and told her how our attempts had failed. She spoke bluntly, assuring me that she could let us have exit visas valid for one month; for the five remaining months I would have to approach the Rumanian embassy in Paris. She named her price and told me that she was making a trip to the West at the beginning of March 1969. If she received the money she had asked for during her stay, our passports and visas would be granted as soon as she returned to Rumania at the beginning of April. Something told me that she meant what she said, and I decided to give it a try. I discreetly warned my friends in Paris, and they did what was necessary, leaving the money at the woman's hotel. As soon as she returned to Rumania we were summoned to the passport office, where we received two passports and two thirty-day tourist visas. The French visa had been obtained some time before. The next day, all formalities completed, we took the first flight for Paris and on April 5th, 1969, we landed at Le Bourget airport. Once in France we asked for political asylum and began a new life thanks to the hospitality and freedom our second homeland offered.

Some months later our close friend arrived in the West with his wife. He told us the astonishing news that the strange lady had also fled to the West with her 'friend', who had held a top job at the central passport office. It was whispered in Rumania that their little schemes had come to the attention of the authorities, and that, forewarned, they had fled before the secret police could arrest them.

Apart from our friend no one, not even our families, had any idea that we intended to settle for good in the free world. Those dear to us have waited years for us to return so that we might meet again. My poor mother died in 1973, cherishing to her last breath the hope of seeing us once more.

This separation from our families, and in particular our hasty departure, will always be a barb in our souls.

We are doing our best to justify this sacrifice, by our constant efforts to promote our faith. The Lord watches over us.

Judy Wurmbrand

ESCAPE FROM THE GRIP

A Jewish girl's discovery of Christ and freedom.

This is the autobiography of a young Romanian-Jewish girl. In Judy the spark of freedom will not be extinguished. She learns early in life how to survive and preserve her identity under an all-pervading dictatorship, in the shadow of the secret police. At last, her family find a way to leave the country they had loved.

To a great extent all is triggered off by her childhood neighbour, Michael Wurmbrand (son of the legendary Pastor Richard Wurmbrand, fourteen years imprisoned for his faith). Years later, while in Israel, separated from him, she embraces the Christian faith and later marries Michael.

Hermann Hartfield

IRINA

A love stronger than terror. A faith stronger than death.

Many Christians in the West talk about dialogue with Communism. Irina led a group of Christians in Russia who tried it. After initial encouragement from the authorities, the result was imprisonment. But Irina refused to deny her faith. Her extraordinary story is the central thread in this gripping revelation of everyday life for Christians in Russia today, combining suspense and adventure, triumph and persecution, joy and suffering. More than this, it is the compelling story of a love that would not give up, finally uniting Irina with Sasha, a young Baptist preacher.

Hermann Hartfield was imprisoned in Russia on three occasions for a total of seven years as a result of his role in the secret church. He was finally deported to West Germany, where he now lives.